D1301151

THE POWER OF ONE

One Person, One Rule, One Month

John C. Maxwell

with

Stephen R. Graves
Thomas G. Addington

NELSON REFERENCE & ELECTRONIC
A Division of Thomas Nelson Publishers
Since 1798

www.thomasnelson.com

Copyright © 2004 by Maxwell Motivation, Inc.

All rights reserved. No portion of this book may be reproduced, stored in a retrieval system, or transmitted in any form or by any means—electronic, mechanical, photocopy, recording, scanning, or other—except for brief quotations in critical reviews or articles, without the prior written permission of the copyright owner.

Printed in the United States of America

04 05 06 07 VG 7 6 5 4 3 2

ACKNOWLEDGMENTS

Three people really helped make this book and its deadline possible. A mixture of astonishment and appreciation fill my heart for you.

Andrew Brill
Sam Hannon
Sarah A. Moser

Thank you for the time-compressed effort you provided in research, brainstorming, writing, and editing. You guys kept this project from being a finish-line failure.

I'm only one, but still I am one.
I cannot do everything, but still I can do something;
And because I cannot do everything
I will not refuse to do the something that I can do.

—Edward Everett Hale
Quoted in
The Power of Character,
Michael Josephson, ed.
(Jossey-Bass: 1998), 14.

Contents

OWNERS GUIDE

This is a workbook. It is intended to be marked up, the cover soiled, pages wrinkled and folded down, and well-used like an old pair of Birkenstocks. It should become an ethical journal of sorts. This is not a coffee-table picture book. It is not a fun, action-filled novel that you speed your way through with a bowl of popcorn, then retire it to the shelf. It is not an academic book that will take a few years to wade through, and even then only a select few will understand it and find use for it. It is a workbook, a manual, a field guide to any person hoping to make and leave a mark of positive influence.

The driving concept for the book is fairly simple: If one person will intentionally take the golden rule, which we refer to as the One Rule, and practice it like a religious zealot for one month, a remarkable thing will happen. The ethical watermark will go up in any environment. It will happen in any family, in any company, in any community, and even in any country.

That is the Power of One. One Person, One Rule, One Month.

This book is designed to be a partner to John Maxwell's trade book There's No Such Thing as "Business" Ethics. In his book, John grounded the notion that our ethic and behavior ought to be one consistent demonstration. And that ethic ought to be seamless in all the parts of our lives. There should not be one ethic for one part of our lives (as in business) and another ethic for the other parts of life. There is only One Rule.

Take this workbook and work through it. Read it. Reflect on it. Respond to it. Live it. Become a hero in your company. Become a hero to your spouse and children. Become a hero to your community. Become a hero in today's world and tomorrow's generation. Become a hero to yourself. Be able to look in the mirror and smile, not from arrogance, but from satisfaction and fulfillment. Know that your life counted.

Put into practice the Power of One.

THE POWER OF ONE

The world is moved by highly motivated people, by enthusiasts, by men and women who want something very much or believe very much.

—JOHN GARDNER

DRIVING THOUGHT

The Power of One means that I treat everyone—no matter his or her position in life—as I would want to be treated.

DRILLING DOWN

Mike Abrashoff, author of *It's Your Ship: Management Techniques from the Best Damn Ship in the Navy*, is the epitome of someone who was ready for his golden opportunity when it came and who achieved success by practicing the golden rule. Before Mike took his first command, which was of the USS *Benfold*, he had already been successful. He had graduated from the U.S. Naval Academy at Annapolis. He had excelled as an officer, attaining the rank of captain after sixteen years, and had worked as military assistant to Dr. William J. Perry when he was Secretary of Defense. But when Mike took command of the *Benfold*, he saw it as a rare opportunity to do something different, to use a Golden-Rule approach to leadership. Mike says:

The first sixteen years of my career, I went for the gold braid. I had success, but it wasn't unusual success. The last two I went for the golden rule. I took command of the ship and took command of my life. Before, I was working according to what I thought were the organization's expectations. But while working for Secretary of Defense Perry, I saw a departure from that kind of thinking. When I saw my predecessor leaving the ship, I thought about what my departure would be like.

The navy is like a tree full of monkeys. If you're at the top of the tree, all you see when you look down is a bunch of smiling faces looking up to you. When you're at the bottom of the tree and you look up, you have a different kind of view!

Mike decided to put himself in his sailors' shoes. He interviewed every sailor on his ship individually to find out what they valued, and then he made changes to add value to his sailors. For example, he sent the ship's cooks to culinary school and offered college courses aboard ship. He asked his officers to treat the new arrivals as they would want people to treat their children. And he empowered everyone—officer and enlisted person alike—to make decisions and work to make their ship the best in the Navy, trusting them and encouraging them with the words "It's your ship."

"Good began to happen when I began going for the golden rule," says Mike. "I put people instead of promotion first. And as a result, I was paid a thousand times over." That's what I call making the most of a golden opportunity!

SUMMARIZING PRINCIPLES

1. Practicing the Power of One often requires stepping out from the normal march of conventional thinking and looking at life from a different perspective.

2. I must learn to do things because they are right, not because they might come back to benefit me.

3. It is impossible to practice the Power of One without focusing on other people.

4. Seeing a person practice the Power of One is contagious.

5. Treating others the way you wish they would treat your children, parents, or best friend is a great way to begin practicing the Power of One.

6. Often we have to unlearn certain habits and tendencies when it comes to reacting and treating people the right way.

MAKING EVALUATION

There's no such thing as business ethics—there's only ethics. People try to use one set of ethics for their professional lives, another for their spiritual lives, and still another at home with their families. Circumstantial ethics get them into trouble. Ethics are ethics. If you desire to be ethical, you live using one across-the-board standard.

Mike Abrashoff realized the need for a standard of ethics. And taking charge of his life was critical to his success. So he purposely set some new guidelines and boundaries to guide the way he treats other people. He said, "This is the way I want this to go, and this is the way I want to act." Then he learned to follow those guidelines and reaped the rewards of a well-ordered life.

To further illustrate the need for clear guidelines, think about how a builder erects a house. He doesn't just nail a few pieces of wood together at random and pour cement where it pleases him. He doesn't cut holes into the sheet rock for windows without thinking through the placement. If he did, the result would be a disaster. He builds from a blueprint before the first hammer swings.

Do you have a plan for your life? Have you set boundaries to follow that outline your every move? Mike Abrashoff did. And that's what we need to do in order to live a powerful—and intentional—life.

What motivates you? What fuels your engine to act the way you do, say the things you say, and respond the way you respond?

The other day a friend and I were lamenting the trials that used-car repairs bring to a father. My friend and his son had recently bought a used Honda. As used-car stories go, within a month it needed an emergency-room visit to the local mechanic. The Wrench Doctor diagnosed a bad carburetor. My friend's options: buy a new carburetor, buy a used one, or have the mechanic rebuild the shot carburetor. Or take the advice of his young son.

The nonmechanical young teenager said to his dad, "Well, who needs a carburetor anyway?" The dad shook his head and said, "You must understand that your car *will not* run without the carburetor. It is not the most important thing to an engine, but it is pretty central." They chose a new carburetor and the boy is back on the road.

> *Great minds have purposes, little minds have wishes.*
> —WASHINGTON IRVING

Central to the human machine is the "motivator." That is the piece of internal equipment in all of us that signals our impulse to go a little further than normal, to step in and get involved when we really don't have the time or resources. Our motivator is the seat of our emotions and our wills. It drives our behavior and steers our dreams. It is the thing that fuels our desires, catalyzes our energy, and commands our actions. Without a smooth running "motivator," it is hard to practice the Power of One.

Adjusting Your "Motivator"

Practicing the Power of One often requires stepping out from the normal march of conventional thinking and looking at life from a different perspective. Mike Abrashoff reversed his approach to identifying with his troops. He chose to start from the bottom up, instead of dictating from the top down, by asking his guys what they needed from the ship and what the ship needed from them. Flipping upside down his idea of how to lead people brought great rewards.

His team knew he cared about them; he learned what mattered to them, and hence was able to lead them more easily and provide them with value in their jobs. The bottom line: Mike learned to focus on other people first. And that's the key tenet of practicing the Power of One. He adjusted his motivator so that he was energized by helping others and doing the good, the right, and the true.

When Mike started practicing the Power of One, he realized the need to get in touch with his sailors to find out what they valued. This isn't a new thought, but it isn't always an easy task to accomplish. For example, a CEO buddy of mine makes it a practice to go on a field trip to the different layers of his organization a couple of times a year. He struggles to find the time for this exercise—and often wonders how necessary it is—but he does it religiously anyway. Why? It puts him in touch with the people of his organization in a more personal way. He sees them doing their jobs, interacting in their surroundings. Instead of seeing his workers only at staff meetings where they're prepared to speak in a specific way, this CEO goes into his workers' elements and sees what they really do. And in this exercise he learns more about them, about what they need to better do their jobs, and about the people they serve—something you can't learn sitting in a corner office with no contact with the people below. Does it really pay off to treat people that way? J. W. Marriott Jr., CEO of Marriott International, Inc., thinks so.

That is what made one fellow say that practicing the Power of One really is the Ethical Circle of Life. The Power of One is not complicated at all. It is simply the internal motivation that says I am going to treat you the way I would want to be treated—all the time—regardless.

> *Motivate them, train them, care about them and make winners out of them . . . we know that if we treat our employees correctly, they'll treat the customers right. And if customers are treated right, they'll come back.*
>
> —J. W. MARRIOTT JR.

TAKING ACTION

Launch "Operation Regardless"

"Operation Regardless" is your commitment to treating everyone—all the time—correctly. It is a determination to alter the way you look at people and situations. Many times we operate with a filter that adjusts our responses depending upon the situation or the person we are dealing with. The Power of One means that I treat everyone—no matter his or her position in life—as I would want to be treated.

- Do you have a sliding scale of treating some people one way and other people differently?
- Do some situations push you to slip into unethical terrain?
- Do you treat all people—all the time—correctly . . . regardless?

> *Every revolution was first a thought in one man's mind.*
>
> —RALPH WALDO EMERSON

Regardless of Age or Position

- Are you as consistent with your treatment of new hires as you are the old heads?
- Do you treat the beautiful/powerful people in life the same as those who carry no apparent power?
- Do you give the respect and honor deserved to those seniors in your company and community or do you write them off as space takers?

Regardless of Consequence or Credit

- Sometimes people think they can justify their actions by forecasting the outcome of a situation—kind of like the end justifies the means. Sorry, folks, but that won't fly for the Golden Life. You act ethically *no matter what.* Period.
- Do you only act ethically when it benefits you, rather than a coworker? That doesn't count as ethical living either. Being ethical means being ethical *at all times.*

Regardless Whether It Is a Small Thing or a Big Thing

- Size of action doesn't matter. Being honest does. Don't apply ethics just when working with large sums of money, important customers, and deal-making issues. Apply the same standards across the board, whether it's putting a full sixty cents into the snack box at work or turning in an invoice for an hourly job. The issues are the same; the scale and shadow are the only things that change.

Regardless Whether It Is a Public Thing or a Private Thing

- Sometimes it's harder to do the right thing when it's done in front of a crowd. Peer pressure is alive and kicking, even in the corporate world. Stand up for what's right, even if it means standing apart from your peers. At least it will be for something good and honorable.
- When no one's looking, no one will ever find out, or no one cares, it's easy to pull off immoral or unethical practices. But does that make it any more right? No.

Let's do a scorecard:

How would you rate your "motivator" in these situations? How motivated are you to practice the Power of One with everyone all the time?

Situation—Regardless	Running Smoothly	Needs a Tune-Up	Major Overhaul
• If the person is powerful and important	_____	_____	_____
• If the person is a superior	_____	_____	_____
• If the person is a subordinate	_____	_____	_____
• If the deal is a small thing	_____	_____	_____
• If the deal is a big thing	_____	_____	_____
• If the deal is quiet and in privacy	_____	_____	_____
• If the deal is going to cost me something	_____	_____	_____
• If I get the credit	_____	_____	_____
• If I don't get the credit	_____	_____	_____

Adopt the Golden Ruler

Begin to measure your every action against a single question. Don't overcomplicate it and don't underestimate it. If One Person will take the One Rule and practice it for One Month, amazing moral traction happens. There is no environment where the ethical waterline will not rise. There is something very powerful in doing the good, the right, and the true. The golden ruler measures our conduct against the One Rule. For the next thirty days, ask yourself this question as often as possible: Am I treating others the way I would want them to treat me?

- Take the time to post this Rule in as many places as you can to help steer your thinking toward it. Name five prominent places in your life orbit that you can post the One Rule and leave it there for one month.

> *Communicate downward to subordinates with at least the same care and attention as you communicate upward to superiors.*
>
> —L. B. BELKER

1. _____
2. _____
3. _____
4. _____
5. _____

I have had people say, "The rule works OK most of the time, but you just don't know my particular situation. It is rather complex and complicated." If the Rule doesn't seem to work as effectively as you wish, let me give you three questions that actually stand alongside and even behind the One Rule. If you were to turn the golden ruler over, this is what you would find: three shorter questions of measurement.

- Is it right?
- Is it good?
- Is it true?

Remember, seeing someone practice the Power of One is contagious. Do you believe that? Really? It only takes one person practicing the Power of One to start a trend.

Be that one person. Make a difference.

He who reforms himself, has done much toward reforming others; and one reason why the world is not reformed, is, because each would have others make a beginning, and never thinks of himself doing it. —Thomas Adams

---

Day 2

WANTED: ONE ETHICAL LEADER

When you tell the truth you don't have to have a good memory.

—WILL ROGERS

DRIVING THOUGHT

The Power of One believes that the influence of one person or one idea can alter the whole world in a positive, real way.

DRILLING DOWN

TIME magazine named Cynthia Cooper as Person of the Year in 2002. Why? Because she helped bring peace to some chaotic corner of the world? No. Because she discovered a cure for a terrible disease? No. Because she solved a long-standing scientific question? Again, no. Cooper was singled out for international acclaim simply because she told the truth.

As WorldCom Inc.'s internal auditor, Cooper heard from another executive in March 2002 that corporate accounting had redirected $400 million from one account into another in order to inflate income. When Cooper attempted to determine what had happened, an angry CFO told her to leave the issue alone. Cooper refused, and in the process she uncovered what has since become the largest accounting fraud in history.[1]

Most people are disgusted with the state of ethics in America. They are sick of dishonesty and unethical dealings. University of California Berkeley accounting Professor Brett Trueman, who teaches at the Haas School of Business, remarked, "This is why the market keeps going down every day—investors don't know who to trust. As these things come out, it just continues to build."[2]

That is the bad news. Here is the good news: It only takes one individual who's willing to tell the truth to reverse a negative slide. When that one person steps up to ethical leadership—regardless of his or her position or level of power—then the golden rule takes effect and begins doing its good work. That is what Donald H. McGannon had in mind when he said, *"Leadership is action, not position."* It was for this very kind of thing that Immanuel Kant, the razor-sharp philosopher said, *"So act that your principle of action might safely be made a law for the whole world."*

Cynthia Cooper took the role of ethical leader at WorldCom. Her fellow honorees of *TIME* magazine's 2002 Persons of the Year stepped into similar ethical leadership positions at two other organizations: Coleen Rowley at the FBI, and Sherron Watkins at Enron. All three of those brave women assumed the mantle of the Power of One; all three took heat for their stance as whistle-blowers; and all three have made an enormous and positive difference. Real leaders are ordinary people with extraordinary determinations.

But becoming an ethical leader and following the golden rule doesn't usually involve whistle-blowing. It does, however, always involve telling the truth.

Years ago, Douglas Aircraft Company was competing with Boeing Aircraft Company to sell Eastern Airlines its first big jets. Eddie Rickenbacker, the head of Eastern, reportedly told Donald Douglas that the specifications and the claims that Douglas Aircraft Company made for the DC8s were close to Boeing's on everything except for noise suppression.

Rickenbacker then gave Douglas one last chance to outpromise Boeing on this feature. After consulting his engineers Douglas reported back to Rickenbacker that he didn't believe he could make that promise. Rickenbacker replied, "Oh, I know you can't. I just wanted to see if you were still honest. You just got yourself an order for $135 million. Now go home and silence those jets."[3]

SUMMARIZING PRINCIPLES

1. We encounter ethical leadership "step-up opportunities" on a regular basis—opportunities to do the right thing and tell the full truth.

2. Sometimes taking ethical leadership means standing alone.

3. We are always being watched, and we never know when someone is testing our ethics.

4. Ethical leadership allows us to relax. We don't have to overanalyze, outwit, or even be that much smarter than someone else. We just need to be willing to tell the truth.

5. One person standing up for what is right and true builds retaining walls against entire mudslides of mistrust and wrongdoing.

MAKING EVALUATION

When pollster George Barna asked people whether they had "complete confidence" that leaders from various professions would "consistently make job-related decisions that are morally appropriate," the results were abysmal:

Type of Leader	% Who Hold Public's Complete Confidence
Executives of large corporations	3%
Elected government officials	3%
Film and TV producers, directors, and writers	3%
News reporters and journalists	5%
Small business owners	8%
Ministers, priests, and clergy	11%
Teachers	14%

It's revealing that even regarding the most trusted leaders (teachers), six out of seven people are unwilling to give them their complete trust. There is a crisis of ethical confidence that surrounds entire professions. The public's trust has been shaken.

But the question right here, right now is not about public confidence in an entire profession. It's about me. A Chinese general put it this way: "If the world is to be brought to order, my nation must first be changed. If my nation is to be changed, my hometown must be made over. If my hometown is to be reordered, my family must first be set right. If my family is to be transformed, I myself must first be."[4] Trust in leadership and trust in life starts with one person at a time earning it and practicing it. The real question is, Do you have confidence in yourself to take an ethical stance—even in tough situations? Would others expect that kind of leadership from you? Let's digest that question a little further.

1. Name someone you admire (either an individual you actually know or are familiar with) because he or she always tells the truth, and therefore is someone you can always trust. If you rated his/her word on a scale of 1 to 10, and then did the same with your word, how would you compare?

_____

_____

_____

2. Identify from your recent past a situation in which you needed to show more backbone.

_____

_____

3. Look at your calendar for the next week and practice some ethical anticipation. In other words what specific situations do you see coming your way that will require more than normal moral backbone?

_____

_____

_____

_____

_____

_____

Taking Action

The Power of One is truly astounding. One ethical leader has the power to transform any situation. The following simple movements await any leader in practicing the Power of One.

Step Up

The next time the internal alarm clock goes off signaling the opportunity to practice the Power of One, *do it*. Step up and do that which is the good, the right, and the true. Don't wait for the popular vote to come in. Don't wait for someone else to lead the way. Be the ethical champion. It might be in a quiet room balancing the financial books. Or it might be in the public square making an offer to buy a company. It might be in a restaurant by yourself putting the meal on the company card when it should be on your personal card. It might sound out when you find your boss asking some detailed questions of accountability and your options are to lay it on the line or shade the truth.

Whether someone is looking or not, the next ethical intersection you come to, step up and *make the move*. Take the ethical leadership. It could be a moral intersection, financial intersection, relational intersection, or even a physical intersection. Regardless of the distinction, slow down and appraise the speed you're traveling and make sure you don't miss a chance to practice the Power of One. The famous football coach Knute Rockne said: "One man practicing sportsmanship is far better than fifty preaching it."[5] Step up.

Nail Down

Make a firm commitment to truth-telling and honesty. Look in the mirror and ask yourself a few questions. Go even a step further if possible and get feedback from a friend or coworker. Then:

1. Draw an ethical timeline of your life, identifying precisely when you were at your ethical leadership peak.

2. Analyze your communication and accounting style. Which words best describe that part of your world?

	Very Me	Sometimes Me	Rarely Me
Sloppy	_____	_____	_____
Self-interested	_____	_____	_____
Open book	_____	_____	_____
Slippery and shifty	_____	_____	_____
Accurate	_____	_____	_____
Adequate	_____	_____	_____
Hidden agenda	_____	_____	_____
Simple	_____	_____	_____
Forthright	_____	_____	_____
Complicated	_____	_____	_____
Confusing	_____	_____	_____

3. Describe how others perceive your moral authority. Do you have an affinity for the truth or do you lean into the shady world of half-truths and partial deception? Is that a style you picked up along your personal and professional path? If so, when and where?

_____

_____

_____

_____

4. Write out a Power of One Pledge that outlines your personal commitment to be *the* ethical leader in all the circles of your life. Deciding ahead of time doesn't automatically mean you will execute correctly when afforded the opportunity, but it does tilt the action toward the right direction.

Power of One Pledge:

_____

_____

_____

_____

Sound Out

Sometimes it's lonely to be the person sounding out the voice of honesty and truth. Chances are that every week you see people around you who step up and practice the Power of One. They don't go along with popular opinion; they offer the answer that might ruffle the boss, or they take delicate information to a superior for the good of the company. Become a quiet cheerleader. Drop these ethical people a note or leave them a voice mail, or send them an e-mail and tell them what a great job they're doing by practicing the Power of One. Let them know you saw and applaud their willingness to be an ethical leader. Give them emotional support and reinforce the practice of the Power of One.

According to *The Life of Francis d' Assisi*, Francis once invited a young monk to join him on a trip to the local village to preach. Honored to be asked and excited to learn from the master, the monk accepted. All day long Francis and the monk walked through the streets, byways, and alleys caring for the needs of the poor and helpless along the way. They rubbed shoulders with hundreds of people. At day's end the two headed home. Not even once had Francis addressed the gathered crowds. Greatly disappointed, his young companion said, "I thought we were going into town to preach." Francis responded. "My son, we did preach. We were preaching while we were walking. We were watched by many and our behavior was closely observed. It is of no use to walk anywhere to preach unless we preach everywhere we walk!"[6]

One man practicing sportsmanship is far better than fifty preaching it. —Knute Rockne

Day 3

THE ETHICAL DILEMMA

Those are my ethical principles. If you don't like them, I have others!
—GROUCHO MARX

DRIVING THOUGHT

The Power of One means that I courageously choose the right over the wrong, the good over the bad, and leave the outcome to God.

DRILLING DOWN

Cover-ups are prevalent in today's business world. Executives at Enron, Tyco, and WorldCom all tried to hide any wrongdoing. Oftentimes this action stems from poor personal character.

A poster boy for poor personal character is Robert Torricelli, a former U.S. senator from New Jersey. Torricelli made the mistake of accepting numerous gifts and more than $53,000 in illegal campaign contributions from a supporter—but insisted that he'd done nothing wrong. Breaking the law isn't wrong? When Torricelli dropped out of the race for his Senate seat, he attempted to defend his career. The public wasn't buying it. His response: "When did we become such an unforgiving people? . . . When did we stop believing in and trusting in each other?"[1] Herein lies the key. People are more forgiving and trusting when individuals who make mistakes tell the truth and ask for forgiveness, not defend their wrongdoing as Torricelli tried to do. It's as simple as that. The ability to 'fess up and repent goes a long way.

A better example of ethics comes in the person of Harry Kraemer, CEO of medical supply manufacturer Baxter International. In 2001 when dialysis patients using Kraemer's company's filters started dying, Kraemer recalled the products as a precaution, launched an internal investigation, and hired experts to search for possible flaws. Kraemer could have tried to cover up the problem, denied that it existed, and placed blame elsewhere. So what did he do? He extended his condolences to the families of the affected patients and sought to right a wrong. Ultimately, he pulled the product from the market and shut down that division of the company—at a loss of $189 million.

Kraemer even went a step further and reported the problem to rival manufacturers he thought might experience similar difficulties. He did it because it was the right thing. He did it because it was the good thing. He did it because it was the true thing. Kraemer also recommended to the board's compensation committee that his performance bonus be reduced by at least 40 percent that year.

Kraemer has been described as being relentlessly authentic. "Harry lives his life the way most of us would like to live our lives," says Donald P. Jacobs, dean emeritus at the Kellogg School of Management at Northwestern University in Chicago. "What Harry says he believes in, you can put it in the bank. The way he treats his coworkers is the way he'd like people to treat him."[2]

Kraemer made the best of a terrible situation, with integrity. When Baxter International needed one ethical leader, Kraemer raised his hand and jumped in. That is the Power of One. Who could ask for more than that?

SUMMARIZING PRINCIPLES

1. Practicing the Power of One usually has a price tag connected to it.
2. Sustainable ethics require that top management buy in and everyone be a personal champion.
3. Although calculating the return on ethics isn't always an easy thing, we usually feel and acknowledge it deep in our inner person.
4. One person doing the good thing, the right thing, and the true thing can literally save hundreds or thousands of lives.
5. After practicing the Power of One in doing the good, the right, and the true, we must sit back and not try to overcontrol the outcomes.

MAKING EVALUATION

Why are ethics in such a terrible state? It seems that every time I turn around there's another front-page story of a company in peril—all because someone in leadership practiced unethical behavior. It makes me wonder whether we've *always* been in such a fragile state of ethics but we just didn't get caught, or whether we're sliding downward continually. Did the dam break or has there been a leak for a long time? I'm honestly not sure. Although there are many possible responses to that question, I believe when people make unethical choices, they do so for one of three reasons:

1. We do what is most convenient.

An ethical dilemma can be defined as an undesirable or unpleasant choice relating to a moral principle or practice. A decision or response is stranded between the good and the bad, the right and the wrong, the true and the false; we must pull the trigger. Many times we pull the bad, the wrong, the false because we know making the good decision means paying the price that comes with it. Every decision, whether right or wrong, carries a consequence. Out of convenience, we often go with the dark side of ethics because it is easier, even though the consequence is often worse. That's a risk we're often willing to take.

2. We do what we must to win.

The *Atlanta Business Chronicle* reports that a group of executives at a leading company in Atlanta met to brainstorm ideas for a three-day national conference. As the team shared ideas for different sessions to present, a senior vice president of the corporation enthusiastically suggested, "Why don't we do a piece on ethics?"

It was as if someone had died. The room went silent. An awkward moment later, the discussion continued as if the vice president had never uttered a word. She was so taken aback by everyone's reaction, she simply let the idea drop.

Later that day, she happened to run into the company's CEO. She recounted to him her belief that the subject of ethics should be addressed at the conference. She expected him to agree wholeheartedly. Instead he replied, "I'm sure everyone agrees that's an important issue. But there's a time and a place for everything. The sales meeting is supposed to be upbeat and motivational. And ethics is such a negative subject."[3]

Many people believe that embracing ethics would limit their options, their opportunities, the very ability to succeed in business. It's the old suspicion that good guys finish last. They agree with Harvard history professor Henry Adams, who stated, "Morality is a private and costly luxury."

3. We rationalize our choices with relativism.

Many people choose to deal with no-win situations by deciding what's right in the moment, according to their circumstances. That's an idea that gained legitimacy in the early 1960s when Dr. Joseph Fletcher, dean of St. Paul's Cathedral in Cincinnati, Ohio, published a book called *Situation Ethics*.[4]

A course entitled "The Ethics of Corporate Management," offered at the University of Michigan, says in its description, "This course is not concerned with the personal moral issues of honesty and truthfulness. It is assumed that the students at this university have already formed their own standards on these issues."[5]

But to make ethics work, you must have a plan, set guidelines, and established beliefs on those issues. When left to the moment, you're bound to make the wrong choice, because you're caught up in emotions, fear, peer pressure, and other issues that cloud your judgment. Choose to live ethically—and figure out what that really means—before you're stuck in a life-altering crossroad.

Getting a handle on our ethical tendencies is an important step in practicing the Power of One. Ask yourself the following:

Which of these three thoughts most describes the reason I lean into a wrong decision or behavior?

Doing what is convenient.   Guilty, your honor_____   Not guilty_____

Doing what I must to win.   Guilty, your honor_____   Not guilty_____

Doing what seems right at the moment. Guilty, your honor_____   Not guilty_____

TAKING ACTION

Most of us want to act ethically and do the right thing. But corporate incentives and leadership dynamics can lead the well-intentioned astray. Just ask those involved in the imbroglio at Enron, Tyco, and WorldCom. You see how far good intentions got them.

But no matter how much we want to be ethical, we have to face facts: It's not easy. Really, focusing on ethics just isn't sexy like a year-end company meeting celebrating a stock split or record-breaking profit margins. A seminar on ethics or a sales conference in the Caribbean—you tell me which one you're signing up for. A day of team building with a ropes course or a meeting in the headquarters to review the ethics guidelines of the company?

But ethics are important to personal success, professional success, and the livelihood of a company. Just one error in judgment can cost you your job—in fact, it can cost all of your coworkers a job by bringing down the company. Don't think it can't happen; it can, and it will. If you doubt me, just pull out a week's worth of newspapers. You're guaranteed to find proof. When the center caves in because of unethical practices, it's dangerous and devastating.

I know you know this, but the point here is that you can't practice ethics just once, or just when you feel like it, or just when it will benefit you or your company. You

> *Nothing of worth or weight can be achieved with half a mind, with a faint heart and with lame endeavor.*
>
> —ISAAC BARROW

have to practice Sustaining Ethics—sustaining meaning ongoing, continuous, everyday. What's the best way to make something sustaining? Practice. Lots and lots of practice.

You have to make living ethically a way of life, as John Tyson, CEO and chairman of Tyson Foods did at his company. John had invited us to lead a series of discussions around issues and topics that related to improving workplace culture and personal performance. During the course of our discussions, the topic of ethics came up. We were outlining the way a company ought to guide its moral culture in doing the good, the right, and the true.

Toward the end of the lecture, a man in the back raised his hand and said, "Well, what happens if your boss asks you to do something that is wrong or shady? How do you handle that?"

I paused and was about to respond when John jumped up from the middle of the room and said, "I think that question is really directed to me. Let me take it." John Tyson proceeded to explain that the days of people getting away with such behavior are over. He said that if a person makes such a request, the employee must tell John directly—and let him right the wrong. His point was that a company can't build itself up by tearing it down with unethical leaders. "I will help you navigate that dilemma if in fact it becomes one." He was very clear. He stressed the fact that such behavior is wrong—and that if that was the way someone was operating, those days were over.

> *As scarce as truth is, the supply has always been in excess of the demand.*
>
> —Josh Billings

1. What arenas cause you the greatest ethical dilemmas?

Issue	1 (no tension)	10 (full of tension)
Money matters	_____	_____
Gray decisions	_____	_____
Relationships	_____	_____
Gossip	_____	_____
Work/family balance	_____	_____
Traveling	_____	_____
Hobbies	_____	_____
Time	_____	_____
Corporate culture	_____	_____

2. What does the term "Sustaining Ethics" mean to you?

_____

_____

_____

3. How can a person achieve Sustaining Ethics?

_____

_____

_____

4. Can a company ever achieve Sustaining Ethics? Explain.

_____

_____

_____

_____

_____

LEGAL PLUS

A friend said recently that people who want to live out the Power of One have to commit to a more rigorous standard of ethics than just what the law requires. Do you agree or disagree?

_____

_____

_____

I once found a beautiful table at an estate sale. The style was right, the price was right, and the size was right. The only problem? One of the end table's three legs was wobbly, meaning the table leaned too far to one side—and a drink would have slid right off the table and crashed. And that's what will happen to me and to you if we don't use the three legs of sustainable ethics to support our efforts to live right, moral lives. These are the legs that embrace the legal standards but also take us higher to the spirit of morality and ethics. To keep your "table" of ethics upright, you need:

The Golden Triad

Leg 1: The Good

Every decision is either a choice of the bad versus the worst, the good versus the bad, or the good versus the best. Tapping into the internal monitor of goodness will help any decision go easier.

Although it might be a little unwieldy, usually we can detect the spirit of goodness in the midst of dilemmas. Even if it is legal, ask yourself the question, "Is it good?" Let your heart follow that direction.

Leg 2: The Right

We've already established that doing what is right isn't easy. And it's not always the most appealing option. But doing what is right, even in the face of embarrassment, lost deals, financial setbacks, and lack of professional advancement, will keep you out of legal and moral hot water. Are you saying, "Let your conscience be your guide," you might ask. Sure, for about 98 percent of the time. People argue that we must not just follow our consciences. However, I would argue that, for most of the things in life, a healthy conscience has a radar for right and wrong. An internal alarm goes off when we choose wrong over right.

Leg 3: The True

Is it true? Fully true? Always true? Again, the agenda is to create a standard of living that exceeds the legal system. It doesn't go against the legal standard but rather simply applies a more exacting measurement to the dilemma.

> *Today we are afraid of simple words like goodness and mercy and kindness. We don't believe in the good old words because we don't believe in the good old values anymore.*
>
> —LIN YUTANG

If you don't stand for something, you'll fall for anything.

Day 4

CHARACTER + COMPETENCE = SUCCESS

Hard work spotlights the character of people: some turn up their sleeves, some turn up their noses, and some don't turn up at all.

—SAM EWIG

DRIVING THOUGHT

The Power of One gains strength when I meld my character and competence to exert a single imprint of influence.

DRILLING DOWN

Most of the world thought they had lost a treasured businessman of international repute when Armand Hammer died in December of 1990. He had built Occidental Petroleum into a world-wide powerhouse, and as chairman of the board, he consummated deals while globe-trotting in his private Boeing 727 jet.

He was known as a personal advisor to almost all United States presidents from Franklin D. Roosevelt to George Bush Sr. His Rolodex listed virtually every government head in every country of significance, including the Communist nations that were out-of-bounds to United States citizens during the Cold War era. He enjoyed the company of Prince Charles of Great Britain. He cut exclusive business deals with Lenin, Brezhnev, Gorbachev, and other leaders of the Soviet Union. Hammer even purchased an interest in Arm & Hammer Baking Soda because its name coincided with his own. He won lucrative oil contracts in Libya and collected some of the best art in the world. He sponsored conferences on peace and human rights. Armand Hammer may literally have known more world leaders across a wider spectrum of countries and over a greater span of years than any other human being of his era.

It seems that Armand Hammer's life turned out to be ninety-two years of a carefully crafted charade. From the earliest years of his association with the Soviet Union, he tunneled money into a vast Soviet spy network in the United States. Many of his companies were primarily fronts that allowed him to launder money for the Soviet regime. Hoover's FBI investigated him.

He bought politicians around the world. Bribes and illegal secret deals brought him many of his business contracts.

Hammer used and discarded wives and numerous other women. In one case he arranged for his mistress of the moment to have plastic surgery and change her name so that his wife would not suspect an affair. His father went to jail twice for crimes that Armand had committed. He built one entire business on selling fake art that unsuspecting customers all over the United States thought were genuine articles from the Faberge and Romanoff treasures in Russia. He fathered children whom he would not acknowledge and whom he tried to hide. His last wife accused him of defrauding her of her wealth, and after she died, her estate sued him for $440 million. His own son refused to attend his father's funeral.

Armand Hammer's life was a torrid and tangled mess of promises not kept, obligations not met, and corruption left unchecked. His major problem—he had bad *character*.

SUMMARIZING PRINCIPLES

1. Sometimes it takes a while for rotten character to start stinking.

2. No one steals another person's character. I alone am responsible for my character's future.

3. Sound character wedded with solid competence is a combination of irresistible influence.

4. Over time, a deficient character trait is more costly to a company than a weak skill set.

MAKING EVALUATION

A large bank in northern California started a program to train unemployed people as bank tellers. These individuals were hired and trained with full pay and benefits and were treated as regular employees. After only one year the bank terminated this uniquely worthwhile program, not because of the inability of the participants to learn banking skills and not because of a lack of funding or participant interest. The reason the bank gave for ending the program was the participants' lack of "character."

Bank officials and trainers reported that they could teach banking skills, and the participants demonstrated that they could learn these skills. But too many of the participants were unreliable, failed to show up for training, arrived late, failed to call in when they were not going to be at work, could not take constructive criticism, and lacked initiative. In some cases they were dishonest.

Employers really want both. They want someone who has character and competence, not either/or. "Don't make me choose between them," a friend said. "I will not do it, because I expect to hire both in the same person." The character/competence combination is not a new topic.

As far back as the Old Testament, the double-barreled concept of character and competence has been linked to the broad world of effective leading. Nobody knows this better than King David, who captured in the Psalms his thoughts on leadership. If David were here today—and the *Wall Street Journal* scored an exclusive interview with him—here's what he might say about the Power of One, specifically talking about character and competence:

Interviewer: So, David, how old are you now? And what have you been doing lately? We heard a lot about you a few years ago when you were killing giants and hosting victory parties. And while you were king, we always covered the palace. It seems like you were always on the front page with a different story. Catch us up.

David: Yes, I am getting into the years, but I've had a good life. I'm proud of most things in my life, but still have a couple of scars that sting my conscience from time to time.

Interviewer: You have a very colorful résumé. You've been a shepherd, a fugitive, a writer and musician, a military general, and even a king. How has your leadership philosophy changed through the years?

David: Naturally, I've grown more capable and mature through the years. But for the most part, the way I handled my sheep is the way I handled people.

Interviewer: What do you mean?

David: There are two parts to effective leading. It takes heart and it takes hands, meaning character and competence. As a matter of fact, during one of my writing phases I wrote a number of songs. Psalm 78 captures this idea perfectly.

I remember sitting out on a rock one afternoon reflecting on my life and the lives of the people who were under my care. I ended the song with a statement of my leadership intent. It was my Power of One manifesto in ballad form.

So he shepherded them according to the integrity of his heart, And guided them by the skillfulness of his hands. (Psalm 78:72)

Interviewer: Which is more important, the heart or the hand? The character or the competence?

David: You can't divide them. To separate them would be like saying, Which is more important, lungs or brain? It takes both to be alive and influential.

Interviewer: OK, I see. Will you tell us more?

David: Sure. Every person has two things to bring to the job. He or she must exhibit the skills necessary to do the job, and he or she must bring character.

When I was a military general I needed someone to go out on missions that would take a couple of days. This person's job was to secretly penetrate the enemies' territory and gather information on how many soldiers they had, the kinds of weapons they used, and how much food they'd stored up. These issues meant the difference in winning or losing many troops. I needed someone who could count accurately, see clearly, and remember the right things. That's the hand, or competence, I'm talking about.

One thing some of my men failed to understand is that not only must you have competence to get a job, but you must also stay competent to finish the job. Lifelong learning is a really big thing with me.

Interviewer: I think I understand your commitment to competence. How about the other leg of the idea? Tell us a little bit more about character.

David: Sure. Let's take the same examples I gave you earlier. I have to be able to trust the men I send on scouting missions. Specifically, I wanted people I knew would return from a mission, not get lazy or discouraged and give up. And I couldn't send someone who was loose lipped. These missions were top secret.

But, you understand, character without competence just won't do. Some things are meant to be combined, not separated. That's how I feel about character and competence. We get our best imprint when they are both into play.

> *In a new era for business, CEOs face a new mandate. Glamour and glitz are out. Transparency—in terms of ethics, values, and goals—is in.*
> —EXECUTIVE RECRUITERS HEIDRICK AND STRUGGLES

Did you have any idea this kind of emphasis was going on thousands of years ago? Rather surprising, isn't it? But every society rides up and down with the trends and styles that shape everything from our clothes to how we structure our companies. The good news is that Attila the Hun is out. The Jimmy Hoffa style of management is not good today: "*I do unto others what they do unto me, only worse.*"

King Solomon of ancient Israel, reputed to be the wisest man who ever lived, said it this way: "The ways of right-living people glow with light; the longer they live, the brighter they shine. But the road of wrongdoing gets darker and darker—travelers can't see a thing; they fall flat on their faces" (Prov. 4:18–19, *The Message*).

So what exactly is character? Character is the sum of my behaviors, public and private, consistently arranged across the spectrum of my life. *Character* comes from the Greek word describing a marking and engraving instrument. An artist wears a groove on a metal plate by etching in the same place with a sharp tool. Character, essentially, is a habit. I forge my character as a set of distinctive marks that, when taken together, draw a portion of who I really am.

The combination of character and competence is the one-two punch in modern business life.

TAKING ACTION
Success = Character + Competence

If character and competence both play a key role in our success, then it would be wise to take a few minutes to consider how to increase your effectiveness in each area.

Character—This is the "being" part of your life; this is who you are.

Assess your character.

Name three of your character strengths:

1. _____
2. _____
3. _____

Name three of your character weaknesses:

1. _____
2. _____
3. _____

Build your character.

Name some ways you can strengthen your character:

_____
_____
_____

Who do you think of as a character role model or potential mentor in your sphere of influence?

_____
_____

What would a character goal look like for you?

_____

_____

_____

_____

_____

Guard your character.

Work through the following action strategies designed to prevent a character failure, then write a brief application for your context:

- *Be disciplined:* Consistently do the right thing.
- *Avoid temptation:* Try to stay away from compromising circumstances.
- *Seek accountability:* Invite others to ask you tough questions.

Competence—This is the "doing" part of your life.

Assess your competence.

Name three skill areas of strength:

1. _____

2. _____

3. _____

Name three skill areas of weakness:

1. _____

2. _____

3. _____

> *A reputation of a thousand years may be determined by the conduct of one hour.*
>
> —JAPANESE PROVERB

Build your competence.

Take each of the three above-mentioned competency weaknesses and list one way to begin to build some skills in that area.

	Weakness	Competence developer
1.	_____	_____
2.	_____	_____
3.	_____	_____

Improve your competence.

How can you make your strength areas even stronger?

_____

_____

_____

How can you capitalize on your skills to be even more successful?

_____

_____

_____

_____

_____

*We make our decisions and then our decisions
turn around and make us.*

Day 5

ONE RULE FOR EVERYONE

We are members of one great body planted by nature in a mutual love, and fitted for social life. We must consider that we were born for the good of the whole.

—SENECA

DRIVING THOUGHT

The Power of One means that regardless of my background or station in life, the golden rule shapes how I think and what I do and can be applied to everyone . . . everywhere.

DRILLING DOWN

Fiorello H. La Guardia, New York City's mayor in 1935, didn't have to be so kind. But something in him—a powerful Power of One urge maybe—led him to do so one night in the poorest area of New York City, where he presided. According to *Our Daily Bread* (April 4, 1992), La Guardia showed up in court and sent the other judge home for the evening.

Taking the bench, La Guardia learned that his first case involved an elderly woman who was arrested for stealing bread. He asked her whether she was guilty. He heard, "I needed the bread, Your Honor, to feed my grandchildren." The mayor had to punish the lady. "Ten dollars or ten days in jail," he said.

With those words the judge put $10 into his hat. He then fined every person in the courtroom 50 cents. The reason? Because they all lived in a city "where a grandmother has to steal food to feed her grandchildren." In all, La Guardia collected $57.50—enough to pay the woman's fine and send her home with some extra money.[1]

La Guardia could have been harsh and demanded that the woman go to jail if she couldn't pay the fine. But kindness was strong in him. He felt compassion, and he acted. How often have you used your position of power to do good? Does your goodness extend to everyone . . . everywhere . . . or just a select few?

SUMMARIZING PRINCIPLES

1. The golden rule can be used by everyone and can be used *with* everyone.

2. Everyone desires respect, trust, and understanding.

3. There is no one too little or too dirty to receive goodness and kindness from us.

4. Dealing with some personality types seems to bring more of a challenge in living out the golden rule.

5. The baggage we bring to the world of Relationship Dynamics shapes the way we approach, treat, and respond to people.

6. Sometimes practicing the golden rule is hardest with people closest to us.

7. Don't let success or failure harden your heart or blind your perspective toward others.

MAKING EVALUATION

The golden rule can be used *by* everyone and can be used *with* everyone. Do you believe that? We do. Few principles in life provide such universal guidance. Fred Smith Sr., the founder of Federal Express, is one of my mentors. Many years ago he pointed out that a version of the golden rule exists in just about every culture.

That statement stuck with me. It's promising to think that people from every culture who desire to live ethically can agree on one standard. Everyone . . . everywhere can tap into the Power of One. Take a look at the results of some research that show how many variations on the golden rule exist:

Christianity: "Whatever you want men to do to you, do also to them."[2]

Islam: "No one of you is a believer until he loves for his neighbor what he loves for himself."[3]

Judaism: "What is hateful to you, do not do to your fellow man. This is the entire Law; all the rest is commentary."[4]

Buddhism: "Hurt not others with that which pains yourself."[5]

Hinduism: "This is the sum of duty; do naught unto others what you would not have them do unto you."[6]

Zoroastrianism: "Whatever is disagreeable to yourself, do not do unto others."[7]

Confucianism: "What you do not want done to yourself, do not do to others."[8]

Bahai: "And if thine eyes be turned towards justice, choose thou for thy neighbour that which thou choosest for thyself."[9]

Jainism: "A man should wander about treating all creatures as he himself would be treated."[10]

Yoruba Proverb (Nigeria): "One going to take a pointed stick to pinch a baby bird should first try it on himself to feel how it hurts."[11]

What does that grocery list mean? It means there is a commonplace language that everyone understands when looking for harmonious living. That's inspiring. It was Aristotle who coined the phrase "a common place." It became important in his lines of argument and theory on persuading people effectively. A common place is simply the reducing of a situation or issue to the minimum area of agreement—the least thing two people could agree on.

A few years ago I found myself at an impasse with different members of an executive team. We had been invited in to help the CEO and the executive team construct a three-year vision and a one-year path toward tackling some very difficult business realities in their industry. We couldn't find agreement on anything, big or small. So we retreated to baby steps. We looked for and found a common place. It was all we needed to get moving in the right direction.

> *Everyone is a prisoner of his own experiences. No one can eliminate prejudices—just recognize them.*
>
> —EDWARD R. MURROW

Having a tool of connection or a language of understanding doesn't automatically mean we will always remember to use the golden rule. But if we can keep it at the top of our minds, it can help us with everyone . . . all the time. Do you agree that the golden rule can be used *by* everyone and *with* everyone?

One would think that any rule or guiding principle that is that universal would be easy to apply. Our experience has been that for many people there is a gap separating universal opportunity and universal application. What keeps us from applying the Power of One to everyone . . . all of the time?

We all bring baggage to the world of Relationship Dynamics. Many things shape the way we approach, treat, and respond to people. These things can either create bridges or hurdles for us in relationships and activating the Power of One. Specifically, we see four areas that serve as either a bridge or hurdle:

Our Background and Roots

The kind of family we had shapes our RQ (Relational Quotient) tendencies. Every family has its own style of communication, problem solving, celebrating, conflict resolution, codes of conduct, and the like. Be they good or bad, we pick up many early development tendencies and transfer them into adulthood.

The geographic region in which we were raised usually helps frame our RQs. Years ago we hosted a client in our home office. I spent the whole day trying to get this guy to warm up, but he had a prejudice against Southerners that just oozed out of him. Sometimes the area of the world, country, or even the state we grow up in shapes tendencies and prejudices that we need to reverse. If the golden rule is for everyone, we have to shed the filters that barricade people out from the Golden Fountain.

Our Religion and Politics

Religion and politics are supposed to be carriers and enforcers of the good, the right, and the true. Unfortunately, that's rarely true, especially of politics. You'll see what I mean the moment you start talking about presidential races, organized religion, or social issues just about anywhere. One off-base comment about these topics can polarize an entire relationship. Believe me; it's happened more times than I'd like to count.

Our Personalities and Temperaments

Our internal "wiring" plays big in how we treat others and approach issues. A friend of mine says, "You can't change a trait but you can sure change a habit." Boy, that's the truth. He went on to explain that you can't make a person not himself. You can't make Eeyore not Eeyore, but you can sure help Eeyore improve some things. You can teach the person to smile and understand that complaining and being negative doesn't really solve a single problem. You can teach the person that not every day is rainy and cloudy; but no matter what, he will still be himself. You just can't change hard wiring.

Our Habits and Patterns

We are creatures of habits and patterns. We do today what we did yesterday. We respond to a problem today as we did yesterday. We shy away from certain people and move toward other people today the same way we always have. That is because we are creatures of habit. People habits can either be good or bad. We must distinguish between them and try to make changes where necessary.

TAKING ACTION

1. Take a minute and assess your baggage. Would you say the following items are more of a positive bridge for you or a negative hurdle in practicing the Power of One?

	Bridge	**Hurdle**
Background and Roots	_____	_____
Religion and Politics	_____	_____
Personality and Temperament	_____	_____
Habits and Patterns	_____	_____

2. Who are the hardest kinds of people you find to work with and relate to?

_____

_____

_____

Years ago John Trent and Gary Smalley created an analogy to describe different personality styles in people. It was built around the mental image from four common animals. It is another angle at seeing the huge diversity in the word *everyone*. See if you can identify your primary style of behaving.

- *The Beaver*—The busy, task-oriented person. Very focused and challenge-driven. Can work alone or with someone.
- *The Lion*—The classic Type-A, king-of-the-jungle person. Used to being in charge and pretty well sees himself or herself at the top of the food chain.
- *The Otter*—What a party animal. This person really is most motivated when the people factor is at the highest and the fun factor breaks the gauge.
- *The Golden Retriever*—Very compliant. Very loyal. He or she always will be there for you and ready to help. Not a lot of bark or bite.

I liked their analogy. But it just doesn't cover all the people I know. And based on that list, none of us should have much trouble applying the golden rule to everyone . . . all the time. However, have you ever met any of these animals away from the zoo?

- *The Sloth*—This person is one big bag of laziness. He seems to have little to no internal drive—and he lets everyone else do the work. The sloth just clings to coattails and has no interest in independence.

- *The Piranha*—This person has a vicious, deadly bite. She runs in a circle of sarcasm, accusation, blame, and foul language.
- *The Alligator*—The alligator sits in the water looking peaceful and calm. But look out—one false move and he'll explode with violence and revenge.
- *The Elephant*—This person lumbers along and doesn't seem to have a clue about the little things of life. What path? What plan? She tends to go on her merry way, participating when the mood strikes. Others have to manage over and around the elephants—or risk getting stepped on.
- *The Porcupine*—This person seems to have so many prickles that no matter where you touch him or her, you end up getting bloody. The porcupine is high maintenance and always demands that you approach with extra grace and measure.
- *The Jellyfish*—This person looks like shelter, glows in the water, and appears to be the one you can cling to. But once you're close, you get stung.
- *The Monkey*—The monkey likes to be in control and fails to trust or empower others. He micromanages—nitpicks—you and is never happy with your performance.

3. What other animal caricatures come to mind in your dealings with people?

_____

_____

_____

_____

_____

4. Now that the list is expanded, think again. What personalities are the most difficult for you to do the good, the right, and the true with?

_____

_____

_____

5. If my family and close friends were going to label me with an animal caricature, what would it be?

———————————————————————————

———————————————————————————

———————————————————————————

———————————————————————————

———————————————————————————

Unfortunately many of us need to unlearn some habits, especially with those people we're closest to. With family, friends, and coworkers, it's easy to slip into a mind-set that, quite frankly, becomes dull and lazy in relationship dynamics. We call this RQ (Relational Quotient) in our executive life coaching.

6. Why do you think we many times treat those closest to us worse than we do a total stranger or an acquaintance?

———————————————————————————

———————————————————————————

———————————————————————————

———————————————————————————

How much improvement do you need to make in this area?

1. I'm a slight offender.
2. I'm definitely getting worse and trending the wrong way.
3. I need some serious adjustment.

One of the first rules in human relations is to seek common ground with others. That's a good guideline whether you are exploring a new friendship, meeting with a client, teaching a student, connecting with children, or arguing with your spouse. Comparing similar experiences and discovering shared beliefs can pave the way for successful relationships. The golden rule can be used to create common ground with any reasonable person.

———————————————————————————

I learned that it is the weak who are cruel, and that gentleness is to be expected only from the strong. —Leo Rosten

———————————————————————————

Day 6

One Rule for Everything

If you are standing upright, don't worry if your shadow is crooked.

—Chinese proverb

Driving Thought

The Power of One means there is never a situation or setting in which the golden rule can't help.

Drilling Down

Countless children and their families traipse through the Jones Center for Families in Springdale, Arkansas, each year. They host birthday parties, take a swim, skate around the rink, attend church services, and use the computers at the facility—all for free, and all thanks to the late Bernice Jones.

That doesn't even begin to describe what Bernice, who died at age ninety-seven, did for her community. To be fair, many people don't even know about the way she affected her community for good—she preferred to keep her giving and financial information as private as possible. But we do know that she and her late husband, trucking magnate Harvey Jones, set up a lifetime of giving—without expecting a thing in return. And the most remarkable element of their giving was that it targeted a huge diverse swath of people and things.

During the Great Depression, Harvey and Bernice rented a building, hired a teacher, and paid for supplies to keep the Springdale School District open. In the 1950s they helped develop the city's first hospital; in 1992 Bernice pledged $25 million to a local medical center.

Students also benefited from Bernice's Power of One. When she could have kept her riches for herself, she instead paid for computers and Internet access for the entire Springdale School District; she established a school of fine arts, and a center for community design at the University of Arkansas School of Architecture in Fayetteville; and many, many more things no one but the recipients of her kindness—if even they—know. And that's the way she wanted it.

She sounds like a wonderful person. And many people say they'd be like her, too, if they had her money. But that's not true. Bernice had a heart of gold *in spite of*, not *because of*, her money. She knew that she could make a difference in many people's lives, and that's what she set out to do. She understood that by giving so freely of her time, energy, kindness, money, and compassion, she could improve one life at a time. She poured her Power of One into all sorts of people and all sorts of things.

You may not have the financial resources of Bernice Jones. But you do have the opportunity to make a difference. The Power of One knows no financial bounds, no age restrictions, no life-position rules. It only knows one person helping one other person.

Are you the person helping—or the person waiting to be helped?

SUMMARIZING PRINCIPLES

1. The golden rule governs both complicated and simple situations.
2. The golden rule navigates in big things and small things.
3. The golden rule advises on both public matters and private matters.
4. The golden rule prevails whether the path is clear or cloudy.
5. The golden rule applies to painful things as well as pain-free things.
6. The golden rule instructs us in money items, relationships, and time concerns.
7. The golden rule escorts us in everything.

MAKING EVALUATION

There are very few things in life that add value to any and every situation. Ordinarily, something that benefits you in one situation might hurt you elsewhere. For instance, gasoline is great for your car, but not so great during a house fire. A winter coat is great during a heavy snow, but useless on the Fourth of July.

You might argue that money always helps any situation. But would it help you buy something on the moon? I think not. Few things in life have universal value.

Some friends of mine started a new company recently to identify and place new products into mass retail. One of the founders joined me in taking our sons on a father/son camp. This man always loves to show off the latest breakthrough invention his company is working on. The weekend camp was the perfect stage to test this universal one-size-fits-all headgear called a Zub. This headgear works as a do-rag, bandanna, headband, face mask, and many other things. All told, their marketing campaign shows sixty-nine different uses. How can it be so versatile? Simple: one size fits all.

So one night our whole cabin, dads and sons alike, donned Zubs. We were a walking advertisement for this guy. There were old heads and young heads, small heads and large heads. Long thin heads, round heads, and honestly, one guy even had a square blockhead. We had every kind of head imaginable. The truly amazing thing was that the Zub fit every head. This little piece of cloth was truly amazing.

The golden rule is definitely a one-size-fits-all principle for life. In the last chapter we explored the notion that it can be used *by* everyone *with* everyone. In this chapter we want to develop the idea that the golden rule can be used in everything. In other words, its one-size-fits-all elasticity gives us the freedom to put it to use all the time.

1. Why is the golden rule helpful in all situations?

_____

_____

_____

2. Can you think of a situation where the golden rule would not be beneficial? Couldn't think of one? That's the point. The golden rule benefits every situation—always.

Which of the following best describes your approach to ethics?

- I am always ethical.
- I am mostly ethical.
- I am somewhat ethical.
- I am seldom ethical.
- I am never ethical.

Which of the following do you find easy and which are hard to apply the Power of One rule to?

	Easy	Difficult
Complicated situations	____	____
Simple situations	____	____
Big things	____	____
Small things	____	____
Public matters	____	____
Private matters	____	____

	Easy	Difficult
When the path is clear	_____	_____
When the path is cloudy	_____	_____
Painful things	_____	_____
Pain-free things	_____	_____
Money items	_____	_____
Relationships	_____	_____
Time concerns	_____	_____
Everything	_____	_____

Some of us are more of a situational ethicist than we might first think. Our standard of good, right, and true varies from situation to situation. But having an ethic that fits every situation makes life easier—and keeps you out of trouble.

My daughter announced to me on the way to school one day that she earned a 100 percent grade on the driving test. In front of a carful of her peers I said, "That is so good to hear. As a matter of fact, that's fantastic." Especially because she had failed the test the first time.

I then asked her whether I could expect her to never get a ticket, never get into a wreck, and never have any car trouble. The car got strangely silent. Then she finally muttered, "No, I can't promise that."

My daughter explained that making a good score on the test didn't guarantee no tickets, no wreck, and certainly no immunity from car problems. I laughed and used that as a great teaching moment with my girl and her buddies. Knowing the right answer and doing the right thing aren't the same thing. But certainly knowing the right answer helps.

TAKING ACTION

We begin to experience the Power of One when we live by the golden rule.

Think through the following situations—the Golden Challenges—and determine how the golden rule exposes the ethical choice in each situation:

Golden Challenge #1

A client of yours is looking to buy some of your product. The product's currently on sale, but the client doesn't know this. Is it ethical to complete the order at the original price and make more money for your company, or should you tell the client about the sale price, decreasing company profit? What do you think?

Apply the Golden Rule.

_____

_____

_____

_____

_____

Golden Challenge #2

You have committed to some family activities that will take place in the upcoming weekend. Your children and spouse are not only expecting you to be there, but they are very excited about your presence. Heading into the weekend, you're offered a spot in the company sky box for the big game. It isn't a requirement, but it is a good opportunity to mingle with clients and your boss. Plus, this is the biggest game of the season. There certainly is a way to spin it to your family as company duty. Where should you be, and why?

Apply the Golden Rule.

_____

_____

_____

_____

_____

Golden Challenge #3

You're setting up a reunion with some old college friends. The plans are beginning to come together and you need to make a few phone calls and send a few e-mails to pass on some information. In your busy schedule, it sure would be helpful to knock some of this stuff out during your downtime at the office. And just two weeks ago you were burning the midnight oil on two different projects that really never got counted anywhere. This could be like an evening of the scales. Is it ethical to use company time, phones, and e-mail to do this? What do you think?

Apply the Golden Rule.

_____

_____

_____

Golden Challenge #4

An older lady at the mall is working the cash register. You popped in to pick up a gift and have only a very narrow window to get your errand accomplished during your lunch break. She is too slow, too talkative, too unaware of your sense of urgency, and actually is very unhelpful. Your choices: be late going back to work, abort your mission and figure out a different plan, or ask for a different salesperson to help you. You want to be nice but something has to give. What do you do, and why?

Apply the Golden Rule.

_____

_____

_____

Golden Challenge #5

You manage an employee who isn't cutting it, even after all your attempts to help. You plan on letting him go when his contract expires next month. You are under no legal/contractual obligation to give him notice. You think that if you tip him off, he'll do even worse and cause company morale to suffer. You know that he is about to close on a new house he just purchased. What do you do? Give him notice or not? What is your reasoning?

Apply the Golden Rule.

_____

_____

_____

_____

_____

Golden Challenge #6

You were off to a good start this morning before you arrived at the airport. You weren't even running late. But as you went through the security station, you encountered the Darth Vader of airline security check guards. There is nothing friendly about him. He obviously took too many power pills for breakfast this morning. He spoke loudly, saying repeatedly, "I couldn't care less about your flight time. This is all about you getting through my station, and I will not be rushed." For some reason he picks you out for a detailed search. You are obviously being treated unfairly. What do you do? Do you simply go along with a smile? Do you block him out and obey his silly rule but then purge him from your memory card? Do you take him on and let him know he's not being very helpful? Do you ask to talk to his supervisor? Why or why not?

Apply the Golden Rule.

_____

_____

_____

_____

Golden Challenge #7

You work at a local auto body shop. A family comes in to drop off their SUV for damages and repairs. You forgot to order the parts two weeks before so they would be waiting for the appointment and the family could get their car in one week, as promised. When they drop the car off you know that they will not be able to get their vehicle for three weeks. Do you just sit on that information to keep their business, or do you step up to the plate and disclose the truth, knowing that that might trigger them to take their repair elsewhere? What do you think?

Apply the Golden Rule.

_____

_____

_____

Golden Challenge #8

You are at a restaurant, and while you are eating, the waitress attending your table has to leave for an emergency. Somehow all the tickets get misplaced. One of your meals is cold when it arrives to the table, and on top of that it is horrible. Everyone is gone and there is no way the cashier has any idea what you ordered. Do you account for only the food that was good? Do you talk to the manager? What do you do, and why?

Apply the Golden Rule.

_____

_____

_____

_____

Golden Challenge #9

You're in charge of purchasing. You've just bid out a project to three suppliers. After receiving two of the three bids, you're not getting the pricing you're looking for. You don't have much time left. You know that if you share the price quotes with the third supplier, then they will come in with a quote that will save the company money and you your deadline. What do you do? Why?

Apply the Golden Rule.

_____

_____

_____

_____

_____

The Power of One assumes there is never a situation or setting in which the golden rule can't help out, add value, or guide us toward the good, the right, and the true. It is the ultimate one-size-fits-all for life. It can help me every day in every way.

The Golden Ruler

Because none of us live the same life with the exact same circumstances, we need something we can fit to our specific situations. Pick up the golden ruler and measure every piece of life each situation at a time. This universal measuring device will help you navigate the peculiarities and uniqueness of your own world. The golden ruler is made up of three questions.

1. Is it good?
2. Is it right?
3. Is it true?

Being able to honestly answer all of these questions with yes will make you sleep better at night. A no answer on any of these questions should give you the red flag you need to make you think twice. Doing what's good, what's right, and what's true in all situations will never steer you wrong.

> **We have committed the Golden Rule to memory;**
> **let us now commit it to life.** —Edwin Markham

Day 7

MOST PEOPLE ACCEPT
THE GOLDEN RULE

It has always been the one great ideal of my life to be of the greatest good to the greatest number of my people possible.

—GEORGE WASHINGTON CARVER

DRIVING THOUGHT

The Power of One is the universal currency that delivers ethical behavior in life and work.

DRILLING DOWN

If she didn't understand the Power of One before, then Carolyn Leuner sure knows it now. Leuner, a 2002 Cornell University graduate with a double major in English and government, set out to teach fifth- and sixth-grade science. Four days before school started, her school switched her to kindergarten, of all places.

The challenge of teaching five-year-olds is big enough. But mix in the fact that Leuner was teaching in Intermediate School 151 in New York City's impoverished South Bronx neighborhood and that she wasn't an education major, and you've got a recipe for trouble. Leuner, however, took it in stride—and surpassed just surviving.

Leuner accepted a position teaching in the Bronx as part of Teach for America, an organization that recruits college graduates to devote two years to teach in urban and rural schools in low-income communities—no teaching degree required. Leuner joined the more than nine thousand people who have been a part of TFA for a two-year commitment. And she definitely stands out.

The scene: An old brick building that houses children of all ages. Teachers often had to lock classroom doors to keep out older kids on the prowl, not to mention the fact that many of Leuner's kindergarten students didn't know their colors—or even their full names.

The challenge: Motivate children from vastly different cultural and socioeconomic backgrounds to pay attention and to learn.

The plan: Focus on each child as an individual—essentially, practice the Power of One, one person at a time. Make these children understand that they are each special and capable of learning and succeeding.

For Leuner, that meant entertaining the children to get them to pay attention in the first place. While battling behavior problems and inattention—something all teachers know intimately—Leuner managed to spend time with the children. It was slow going, but by the end of the year, all of her students knew their letters, could add single-digit numbers, and had keyed in on directions.

> *No act of kindness, no matter how small, is ever wasted.*
>
> —AESOP

What made the difference? Patience and an interest in seeing each and every child succeed. Key evidence that Leuner knew the children she worked with: During the kindergarten graduation, she spoke about each child individually, pointing out what made the child special, how the child had improved over the year, and key successes.[1]

One person—Carolyn Leuner—made a difference in the lives of those children. Special attention, love, support, patience, and the desire to help led to each of her nineteen students learning and achieving.

With more than six billion people in the world, just imagine what would happen if each and every one of us was able to make a difference in the life of one other person.

SUMMARIZING PRINCIPLES

1. There are some gestures and behaviors that translate to all people in all cultures.

2. Any of us can make the Power of One personally applicable and immediately practical by adopting the Golden Accessories.

3. Not a day goes by that we can't upgrade our Power of One influence.

MAKING EVALUATION

A few years ago I participated in a two-week research trip around the world. We stopped in a dozen countries exploring a new business idea. To prepare, one of my partners read up on the places we would be visiting. The most obvious challenge was going to be the language and communication barrier. Can you imagine trying to learn enough languages to travel the globe? It's nearly impossible.

My friend, however, found that there are a few common elements of communication in almost all languages. For instance, the hand gestures for *stop* and *go* don't seem to vary much. I'm not sure how much good those did us, but hey, at least we knew them!

This quandary got us thinking. There really aren't too many universal elements of communication. But one that works almost everywhere: a smile. That's right, a good, old-fashioned smile breaks the ice as easily in Africa as it does in Ireland as it does on the street on which you live.

So we tried it. We smiled a lot. And it worked like a charm. It was the ultimate universal traveling accessory.

Golden Accessories

Speaking of accessories, boy, did I get a lesson in accessories when my wife and I built a new house. I thought we were done once we had a building, some furniture, carpet mixed with hard wood, and a little light to live by. But I was wrong.

One day she announced, "We need to get some window treatments."

"Why?" I naively asked.

She explained that the window treatments, pictures, knickknacks, rugs, etc., are critical to pulling the whole room together. "It makes everything complete," she said. "It is called accessorizing."

I guess that makes sense.

She went on to say that it's the same as a woman accessorizing her favorite black dress. The dress looks fine without the pearls or the scarf, but the outfit's complete with the addition of the right shoes, purse, jewelry, hairdo, and makeup.

What is true with home accessorizing and fashion accessorizing equally applies to the Power of One. Try on these Golden Accessories:

A Smile

Tim Sanders writes in *Love Is the Killer App*, "Think about what I call soul smiles. Everyone knows how to smile, although many flash a fake grin that is worse than no smile at all. People can tell when that flash of teeth is a lie. Some people smile, however, from their soul. It feels as comforting as when close friends hug you after a long absence. Smiles have that same effect when you take the time to think about them, when you let them radiate from deep within."[2]

It just doesn't take too much to turn the corners of

> *Flattery is from the teeth out. Sincere appreciation is from the heart out.*
>
> —DALE CARNEGIE

your mouth up. All it takes is for your mind to flip the switch and send a command to "turn up the corners." And there you have it. You don't have to be completely pleased with everything going on around you or in you. But if you will offer a smile that is genuine to someone and frame the smile with friendly eyes, you will begin the Power of One momentum.

A Thank-You

Let's admit it: Those two magic words usually trigger the first golden accessory—the smile.

You can work night and day on a project, striving to get everything right. You put in extra hours, suffer stress in the process, and turn in what you think is your best work yet. But what happens when your boss fails to thank you for your extra effort? You're crushed.

> *There's a self-expansive aspect of gratitude. Very possibly it's a little known law of nature the more gratitude you have, the more you have to be grateful for.*
>
> —ELAINE ST. JAMES

Instead, what happens when your boss sends you an e-mail glowing with praise, or swings by your office (or cubicle, more likely) and simply says "thanks"? He or she has made your day. And the long hours, meticulous work, and compromises you made were all worth it.

Don't deny someone—anyone—the power of a sincere expression of thanks. Doing so will do more damage to that person's self-worth—and to yours—than you know possible.

Eye Contact and Focus

Few things are more important to people than knowing that someone genuinely recognizes them and sees them for who they really are. Probably the easiest way to signal that affirmation is eye contact. We live in a hurried, distracted world. Practice providing relational focus. It's a Golden Experience.

"Television has proved that people will look at anything rather than each other," writes Tim Sanders. " People look at foreheads, eyebrows, noses—anything but the eyes. So I try to make it happen. If I have to, I take my hands and grab someone's shoulders to stop both of our worlds long enough to make true eye contact. It is the strongest way to bond. It shows you are present and you care."[3]

Not sure of the importance of eye contact? If you're a parent, you surely know how it feels (or felt) when your young child crawls into your lap and grabs your face. Why does your child do it? To get your attention. To be validated. Adults can't do the same act to get your attention, but the same desire is there. Grant it.

Remembering a Person's Name

Dale Carnegie once remarked, "Most people find there's no sound more beautiful than the sound of their own name." I became convinced that remembering someone's name was very important when I was working as a truck driver for a moving company during my doctoral studies. People always referred to me as "Driver," no matter how many hours I'd been with them, helping them load the truck and move.

The problem wasn't that they didn't know my name. They did. I'd told them many times. They just chose to not acknowledge me as a person with a name. They just saw me as "Driver."

What does it do when someone calls your name?

> *We should ever conduct ourselves toward our enemy as if he were one day to be our friend.*
>
> —JOHN HENRY NEWMAN

- It establishes warmth and intimacy.

- It combats the impersonal world.

- It heightens your chance of persuasion.

- It communicates care.

Exhibiting a Gentle Spirit

Gentleness, goodness, and self-control are all in the same family of ideas. And good news for those of you who don't find that gentleness comes naturally: It's more of a learned trait than a personality wiring. That means there's hope for all.

Being gentle is about learning to act and react in a nondestructive way. For instance, after a hard-nosed discussion with an employee about her work performance, a gentle spirit will still treat you kindly. She'll be fair and honest and understand where you're coming from—even if it's not what she wanted to hear.

Don't get me wrong; being gentle doesn't mean that you let people walk all over you. It just means that you stand up for yourself in a kind, quiet, and respectful way. A gentle person addresses issues, not people; problems, not personalities.

Listening with Your Heart

Your eyes and mind let you read the words on the page; your heart allows you to read between the lines. And you'll experience these between-the-lines moments all the time. You just don't realize it because you've trained your heart and mind to respond one way or another. The key is getting your heart and mind to read the positive in a situation. Give the benefit of the doubt. And let your heart tell you when something you're about to do or say—or not act on—is unethical.

Your heart can become a radar for the subtle nuance of the ethics of any situation. It usually is where the first alarm will go off that you are encountering something that is bad instead of good, wrong instead of right, and false instead of true. It's also where the violation begins for an ethical failure spiral. Once you start on the slippery slope, it's hard to pick yourself up again.

So train your heart to think about whether each and every situation is good, right, and true. If it's not? Run. Run far, far away. Or at least brace yourself for a stand.

Keeping Your Word

Keeping your word is a powerful—and sometimes quiet—way of practicing the Power of One. For what good is your word if you don't keep it?

Seriously, you give your word that you'll do something, say something, not say something, whatever, dozens of times each day. But do you really stick to all of those agreements? Whether you have a contract or not, your word is binding—and you need to treat it that way.

By keeping your word, you'll show others how one person following through on a promise can make a difference. Who knows—the promise you kept might be the promise that spurs you—or someone else—on to greatness.

> *Losers make promises they often break. Winners make commitments they always keep.*
> —DENIS WAITLEY

Asking Questions

This one might strike you as strange. Asking questions is a Power of One accessory? Sure it is. Questions always open up a monologue and allow for a dialogue. A good question can change the whole direction of a deal. Asking a question is a way to identify all of your options in facing moral and ethical dilemmas.

Do yourself a favor. Ask questions. Compare the answers to the golden ruler—is this new endeavor or friend good, right, and true? Three yeses mean a green light.

TAKING ACTION

The Power of a Smile

1. Would you say that you smile a lot or a little or not much at all?

2. Who in your world is accessorized with a radiant soul smile that really brightens up your day?

3. Try tomorrow to smile more and see what happens. To remind yourself, write "smile" on an index card. Or, if you're more technologically inclined, make yourself a note in your PDA. Take note of how others respond to your cheerful self, and even to how it affects you. Who knows? You might even be able to lower your blood-pressure medication dosage!

The Power of a Thank-You

1. Make a list of the top ten people you're genuinely thankful for. Commit to sending them a "Just *thanking* of you" e-mail or note in the next three days. It will only take a couple of minutes. Start by listing the ten people here:

_____

_____

_____

_____

_____

_____

_____

_____

_____

_____

_____

2. Set up a file in your computer called "Thank-Yous"; file away the notes you sent (above) as well as any that you receive from others. The next time you're feeling useless or overlooked, check your file for encouragement. Then encourage someone else by sending a few more thank-you notes. That other person may be feeling down, as well, and your note will serve as his or her pick-me-up.

The Power of Eye Contact and Focusing on Others

1. Rate yourself: How good are you at making eye contact with others? Would your spouse and colleagues agree with the ratings you give yourself?

Very good   **Average**   **Horrible**

2. Golden Experiment. Identify the three people in your work circles who are best at engaging others with their eyes. What could you learn from these people? Paying attention to how they do it will not only teach you a thing or two, but will also force you to make eye contact yourself. What a deal.

The Power of Remembering Someone's Name

1. How often do you have to ask for someone's name behind his or her back at a meeting or party? If it's often, then you need to determine which of your friends or work associates does a great job remembering names. Ask this person for tips or techniques to help you improve.

2. Can you think of anything you could do right now to improve? Write down your ideas, or the names of those you'd like to ask, below.

_____

_____

_____

_____

3. Pick one person a day and determine to commit his or her name to memory.

The Power of a Gentle Spirit

1. Would you describe your style as a bull in a china closet—or something of a more delicate spirit? Why?

_____

_____

_____

_____

2. When does a gentle spirit just not work so well for you?

_____

_____

_____

_____

3. Does evidencing a gentle spirit mean that you aren't firm or that you don't stand up for a position?

_____

_____

4. Name two people who are beautifully accessorized with a gentle spirit.

_____

_____

The Power of Listening with Your Heart

1. Is your heart in tune with the people and circumstances around you? How can you tell?

_____

_____

_____

2. Do you think you understand this accessory? Why or why not?

_____

_____

_____

3. How can someone improve this area?

_____

_____

_____

The Power of Keeping Your Word

OK, the truth comes out. How many promises have you made today? Keep track. Write your promises, agreements, and plans down. Then follow how closely you follow through on your word. Is it 100 percent of the time? Fifty percent? Or something even more dismal?

If it's anything less than 100 percent, you need work. Start by doing something as simple as writing down your commitments—no matter how big or small—on a daily calendar or in your electronic reminder system. Then check each day that you've kept your word.

Keeping promises is important to building your character, showing that you're trustworthy, and in following through in helping others out. People are counting on you. Don't let them down.

The Power of Asking Questions

Here's an easy assignment: Next time a colleague, business associate, or friend asks something of you, don't say yes immediately. I'm not trying to talk you out of helping others; that's far from my intention. Instead, I want you to learn to get the details on every situation before you commit to something that would hamper your Power of One.

After getting the details, ask yourself:

1. Is it good?
2. Is it right?
3. Is it true?

Too often we underestimate the power of a touch, a smile, a kind word, a listening ear, an honest compliment, or the smallest act of caring, all of which have the potential to turn a life around.
—**Leo Buscaglia**

Day 8

THE GOLDEN RULE
IS EASY TO UNDERSTAND

*Educators, philosophers, theologians, and lawyers have taken what really is a
simple matter and made it very confusing. Living an ethical life may not always
be easy, but it need not be complicated.*

—JOHN MAXWELL

DRIVING THOUGHT

The Power of One is easy enough for a child and tough enough for an adult.

DRILLING DOWN

It's one of the first things you learn as a child: Treat others the way you'd like to be treated. So
how is it that, as adults, we still need to be reminded of this concept? The idea of the Power of
One is really so simple. Kids get it, adults get it, but we all forget to act on it from time to time.
Here's a powerful reminder.

In the 2001 movie *Pay It Forward*, a child takes it upon himself to practice doing good deeds.
Trevor, played by Haley Joel Osment, responds to a homework assignment with this idea: Do
three good deeds for other people, then watch the goodness spread. He timidly approaches the
chalkboard in the front of the class to explain his theory that he calls "paying it forward."
Trevor draws a circle, then attaches three other circles, and then just explodes the visual mul-
tiplication on the board. With every stroke his confidence and enthusiasm builds like a great
conductor surging the orchestra for the final note. At the end he simply lays down the chalk
and goes back to his seat. The teacher, played by Kevin Spacey, and the class sit speechless.

Trevor reasons that, instead of paying him back for helping others, those he helps must pay
it forward by doing three good deeds for three new people. In time, he theorizes, everyone will
be touched by his three good deeds.

While it's true that many good deeds go unnoticed, Trevor's family did get to reap the rewards of his idea. His idea caught on, and the movie finishes with thousands of people, who have been touched by Trevor's life and his idea, standing outside the front door of the boy's modest wooden house. In the background a TV reporter is heard stating that the pay-it-forward idea has spread across the country.

Sure, it was just a movie. But it is a powerful idea. The key? It was simple. It was the kind of thing everyone could understand.

SUMMARIZING PRINCIPLES

1. The Golden Rule: Don't overlook it!

2. The Golden Rule: Don't overthink it!

3. The Golden Rule: Don't overcomplicate it!

4. The Golden Rule: Don't overwork it!

MAKING EVALUATION

One of the wonderful things about the golden rule is that it makes the intangible tangible. You don't need to know the law. You don't need to explore nuances of philosophy. You simply imagine yourself in the place of another person. Even a small child can get a handle on that. There are no complicated rules and no loopholes.

Some things in life have just gotten too darn complex.

My son ordered a scooter off of a Web site. He searched and searched and found a great deal. Unfortunately, what he bought at a low price he paid dearly for in high complexity. He is a young lad with a lot of initiative. His I-want-to-do-it-myself muscle did not go away when he started going to grade school. He ordered the Razorback. It finally came. However, there were no instructions for putting it together. Now get the picture. A giant gas-powered scooter in a box that was too big and heavy for one person to carry. Inside was one half sheet of cryptic instructions in another language.

I could have dropped it off at the closest Nascar Pit

The older I get the more wisdom I find in the ancient rule of taking first things first. A process which often reduces the most complex human problem to a manageable proportion.

—DWIGHT D. EISENHOWER

Crew Training area and I think it would have stumped them. There was such a huge gap between the color picture on the Internet and my son's pulling the string and zipping off to his buddy's house in the next cul-de-sac.

This last summer we were spending a brief break at the beach. We had decided to buy some fresh shrimp and keep them in our condo for the week. I found the name of the closest seafood market and asked downstairs for directions. The guy who gave me directions took me so far out of the way and made the whole trip unduly confusing. My forty-five-minute trip over only took twelve minutes back, once I got good directions!

Do I even need to address the complexity connected with buying your computer over the Internet, then trying to get it serviced over the phone by some fellow sitting in India? Again, some things in life have just gotten too darn complex.

When it comes to the golden rule we should simply follow four guidelines:

Don't overlook it!

Sometimes things can simply slip past us. Simple things can be overlooked because they are not seeking or causing attention. It is the same thing that happens many times in classrooms all over America or in businesses all over the country. The attention all goes to the upper 10 percent or the bottom 10 percent. The overachievers at the top or the troublemakers at the bottom get the attention, and the middle 80 percent go about being overlooked.

> *Too often, our minds are locked on one track. We are looking for red—so we overlook blue. Many Nobel Prizes have been washed down the drain because someone did not expect the unexpected.*
>
> —JOHN TURNER

Don't overthink it!

My kids tell me I have a real gift for overthinking things. I will look at something one way . . . then another way . . . then yet another. The golden rule doesn't need to be overscrutinized. Mark Twain said measure twice and cut once. I usually practice that religiously in life. But in the matter of wielding the Power of One, we should not overthink it. Get out the saw and go to work.

Don't overcomplicate it!

How do we overcomplicate it? By overanalyzing it. By overpersonalizing it. By trying too hard to figure out the chess moves of what-ifs and how-comes.

Don't overwork it!

I once heard a speaker say, "Over time people only implement what they understand and what they buy into."

Soccer's simplicity allows it to be played by young and old. One can find an organized soccer league for a child as young as three years of age. It is so fun to watch them meandering down the pitch, remembering not to use their hands, trying to stay in bounds, and then attempting to kick the ball into the goal. Believe it or not, they can master the simple skills required to play the game well.

At the same time, soccer is played on the professional level by some of the best athletes in the world. Their skills and knowledge of the game are amazing. Watching these men and women play in the World Cup is a really entertaining time. Yet, you will notice they are doing the very same things that a three-year-old does on the field, but on an entirely different level. It is an easily understood game that can be played on any level.

Similar to the game of soccer, the golden rule is a simple-yet-effective ethic. It is simple enough for a child, yet still effective for an experienced worker. Anyone can ask the question, "How would I like to be treated in this situation?" That's not to say that every ethical situation can be solved instantly by using the golden rule. Sometimes the hardest part of asking "How would I like to be treated in this situation?" is identifying who might be affected by the situation and how they might be impacted. But even for complex issues, if a person gives the matter some thought, he or she can almost always figure it out.

1. Explain the golden rule in a simple way. Write it down as if you were going to talk about it to the following different groups. Did you have to make any material content changes or is the rule the same at its core?

Child

_____

_____

_____

_____

Parent

_____

_____

_____

Manager

_____

_____

_____

Employee

_____

_____

_____

2. Why is the golden rule so easy to apply?

_____

_____

3. Do you think the golden rule is too simple? Why or why not?

_____

_____

4. Identify seven words that describe how you wish people would treat you.

_____

_____

The golden rule, then, is taking the list and applying it to myself toward others. It is as simple as that.

TAKING ACTION

Whether it be sports, playing a musical instrument, or driving a car, we get better when we practice the basics over and over again. The Power of One will be fully realized when the golden rule becomes a habit that infiltrates each aspect of one's life. A habit develops through practice and repetition.

Consider taking the following steps in developing the habit of using the golden rule:

Step One – Know the golden rule; memorize it; keep it before you.

Where are three or four different places that you could have a visual presence of the golden rule (for instance, on your refrigerator)?

_____

_____

_____

Step Two – Visualize the golden rule; do some preventive thinking; work through your upcoming situations each morning.

How could you use your PalmPilot or calendar to think through each appointment or task in light of the golden rule before you engage it?

_____

_____

_____

Step Three – Apply the golden rule; choose to act in accordance with the golden rule each day.

As you encounter people and make decisions, you must choose to do the right thing.
Consider this formula for making choices: Ready, Aim, Fire!

READY – pause before you make a choice

AIM – view the choices through the lens of the golden rule

FIRE – make the right choice no matter what the cost

Step Four – Review the golden rule; spend time evaluating your decisions and actions.

Periodically perform a self-evaluation. Ask yourself if your decisions have reflected living by the golden rule.

Periodically ask for evaluation from others. Ask them if you have treated them as the golden rule requires.

Always do right—this will gratify some and astonish the rest.
—Mark Twain

Day 9

THE GOLDEN RULE IS
A WIN-WIN PHILOSOPHY

It is hard for a fellow to keep a chip on his shoulder if you allow him to take a bow.

—BILLY ROSE

DRIVING THOUGHT

The Power of One leaves no losers at the table or victims.

DRILLING DOWN

On the evening of December 11, 1995, wind gusts of forty-five miles per hour pushed wind chills downward in Lawrence, Massachusetts. The same winds fueled flames that raced through the 130-year-old buildings of Malden Mills. For the three thousand employees who worked at Malden, the makers of Polar Tec fabric and fleece, it appeared their jobs had been reduced to a heap of charred rubble.

CEO Aaron Feuerstein's family had operated the mill for three generations. As he assessed the scene, he already knew what he was going to do. With smoke still rising from the ruins, Feuerstein announced that he would rebuild Malden—no big surprise. Then Feuerstein extended a highly unusual gesture: He announced plans to continue paying all employees their full salaries—benefits included—during reconstruction.

Industry leaders questioned the move. Feuerstein spent millions. When asked why, he responded, "The fundamental difference is that I consider our workers an asset, not an expense."[1] Feuerstein obviously understood—and exercised—the Power of One.

So how did Malden's employees respond? Art Boulay of the Organizational Productivity Institute quotes Feuerstein: "Before the fire, that plant produced 130,000 yards (of fabric) a week. A few weeks after the fire, it was up to 230,000 yards. Our people became creative. They were willing to work 25 hours a day."[2]

Feuerstein's generous expression of appreciation was met in kind by his employees. Nearly doubling production in temporary plants set up in old warehouses with an enhanced work ethic to match, the employees found a way to express their appreciation.

The moral of the story: Take care of others, no matter the cost. The goodness just might come back, but even if it doesn't, you must do the right thing. Feuerstein and his associates put the people who work for them before themselves; they put others first.

SUMMARIZING PRINCIPLES

1. Win-win is more than a trendy catch phrase.
2. Win-win has great roots in history.
3. Win-win trades on the good, the right, the true.
4. Win-win doesn't mean equal benefits.

MAKING EVALUATION

The concept of win-win didn't start in America and it didn't begin with this generation. You might be surprised to find that it originally was a part of the thinking that came from Adam Smith. Smith, a Scottish political economist and philosopher, published his Theory of Moral Sentiments in 1759. This work discussed those standards of ethical conduct that hold society together. He emphasized the harmony of human motives and activities in a market setting. Smith is also known for his invisible hand theory, which stated that self-interest is behind much of a nation's economy; public welfare comes second.

Are you putting other people's welfare second? Or are you striving for a win-win environment in which neither you nor those around you have to lose?

Adam Smith believed in win-win 250 years ago. Nothing that has transpired in the last two and a half centuries should make us drift further from that thinking.

Have you met people who believe that in order for them to be winners, other people must lose? They see

> *Our early emphasis on human relations was not motivated by altruism but by the simple belief that if we respected our people and helped them respect themselves, the company would make the most profit.*
>
> —THOMAS J. WATSON JR., IBM

everyone as an enemy who must be crushed. Or they prey on the pain of others in order to win. That seems to be the idea behind a mutual fund that became available in September 2002. It's called the Vice Fund; Mutuals. The fund managers tout it as an investment in "companies that derive a significant portion of their revenues from products often considered socially irresponsible," primarily in gambling, tobacco, alcohol, and defense weapons, industries considered to be nearly recession-proof.[3]

Experts say that such "vice investing" doesn't work and isn't as profitable as investment in "socially responsible" companies.[4] But it's clear even from the name that the appeal of the fund comes from the idea of the investor making money on someone else's weakness. I wonder how the fund manager would feel if he knew people were working hard to exploit his personal flaws for their profit.

> *He that does good to another does also good to himself.*
>
> —SENECA

When you live by the golden rule, everybody wins. If I treat you as well as I desire to be treated, you win. If you treat me likewise, I win. Where is the loser in that? Many times, our culture operates with the mentality that in every situation there is a winner and there is a loser. We love to win and we hate to lose, but everyone hates a tie! But, would you believe it, it's possible for both parties to win, not merely tie.

For example, there can be a win-win situation when you buy a car. Most of us go into the car dealership with our guard up. We want the most for our trade-in, the lowest interest rate, and the rock-bottom price on a car. We want to leave feeling victorious.

Of course, the car dealer wants to maximize his profit. This makes for a competitive environment—obviously, someone will be the winner and someone will be the loser. But what if both parties could win? The car dealer could make some profit and at the same time the buyer could get a nice vehicle for a good price.

Think of it this way: If you were selling the car, you'd expect to make a profit. That's how business works. At the same time, if you're the one buying the car, you want a fair price. If both parties—buyer and seller—understand these principles and treat each other with the golden rule, then both win.

1. What is a win-win situation to you?

_____

_____

_____

2. How does the golden rule help achieve win-win results?

_____

_____

_____

3. Why is the win-win concept foreign to most of us?

_____

_____

_____

4. Why does the win-win concept sometimes feel like a loss?

_____

_____

_____

It's important to point out that every situation actually has three options:

- Best-case scenario. In this case, both parties win. You each give a little, take a little—and you both come out on top. Of course, this works best when both parties are practicing the golden rule, but it doesn't always happen that way.

- OK-case scenario. In this case, one person wins; one person loses. This is the most common case, because it's the way our culture teaches us it should be. Two football teams play; one wins; one loses, just as it should be. Unfortunately, far too often we take that competitive spirit off the football field and into life.

- Worst-case scenario. I don't really need to explain this one, because it's obvious that neither party wins. Why? Probably because they both keep pushing to win—so far that they both just lose.

How do you maximize your share of win-win situations? By practicing the Power of One. By applying the golden ruler—measure every situation by whether it's good, right, and true, and not just for you, but for all parties involved. Treat others respectfully—see their side of the story—and you'll launch the possibility of a win-win. And remember, all it takes is one person to produce a win-win. It doesn't take two people.

Many times we are the benefactors of others' win-win steps. For example:

When Nathaniel Hawthorne, a heartbroken man, went home to tell his wife that he had been fired from his job in a customhouse and confessed that he was a failure, she surprised him with an exclamation of joy.

She said triumphantly, "Now, you can write your book!"

He replied with a sagging confidence, "Yes, and what shall we live on while I am writing it?"

To his amazement, she opened a drawer and pulled out a substantial amount of money.

He exclaimed, "Where on earth did you get that?"

She answered, "I have always known that you were a man of genius. I knew that someday you would write a masterpiece. So every week out of the money you gave me for housekeeping, I have saved something; here is enough to last for a whole year."

> If you have not often felt the joy of doing a kind act, you have neglected much, and most of all yourself.
>
> —A. NEILEN

From her trust and powerful response came one of the greatest novels of American literature—*The Scarlet Letter*. Hawthorne's wife believed in him—and sacrificed of herself to allow him to win. In the end, she, too, won by having a happy and successful husband—and by knowing that she had a hand in bringing about the success.[5]

Of course, every bad job situation doesn't turn into a world-class best-seller story. As a matter of fact, some of them might feel more like a win-lose for a while. But it takes the eyes of confidence and faith to do the right thing and hang on until the harvest comes. It many times takes a while for the good, the right, and the true to germinate and grow.

TAKING ACTION

1. How could a win-win result in the following scenarios?

   • A relationship between a buyer and a seller?

_____

_____

_____

_____

- A relationship between a company and an employee?

_____

_____

- A relationship between a husband and a wife?

_____

_____

- A relationship between two competing companies?

_____

_____

2. What are some of the secondary benefits that result from a win-win for both parties (for example, trust)?

_____

_____

3. Name a relationship in which you could begin to use the golden rule to pursue win-win results. What actions would you take to accomplish this?

_____

_____

4. Have you met people who believe that in order for them to be winners, other people must lose? Have you ever worked for such a person? How did it make you feel and did you ever confront this person?

5. Look at each of the following situations and perform some Golden Analysis. How is there a possible win-win for each of these? Who wins, and how?

• When there is vigorous discussion all around the table during a strategic planning session—and everyone has his or her own points of view.

• When I smile at the janitor on my way out of the office after a long day at work.

• When a friend is honest with feedback regarding my loose actions toward a coworker.

• When my company asks me to do something that I know is wrong and I refuse.

- When my boss gives me a performance evaluation for areas of improvement and I listen and choose to work on those areas.

_____

_____

_____

- When a friend suggests a great book to read and I go on Amazon and buy it and read it.

_____

_____

_____

_____

Always help people increase their own self-esteem. Develop your skill in making other people feel important. There is hardly a higher compliment you can pay an individual than helping him to be useful and to find satisfaction in his usefulness. —Donald Laird

THE GOLDEN RULE IS A COMPASS WHEN YOU NEED DIRECTION

There's harmony and inner peace to be found in following a moral compass that always points in the same direction regardless of fashion or trend.

—TED KOPPEL

DRIVING THOUGHT

The Power of One means that I allow the golden rule to lead me in my life journey.

DRILLING DOWN

What began as a retreat for rest and relaxation on September 10, 1946, ended up as a career in the slums of Calcutta. During a journey to the Darjeeling Mountains in India, Sister Teresa had a clear sense that she should leave her convent, and instead devote her life to living and working in the slums of Calcutta. Such a move would mean a career change. At the time she was principal of a large school, and in order to follow this new vision for the future, she would have to leave both the school and the convent. She requested permission from church authorities, but had to wait until July of 1948 before she received permission. The archbishop gave her twelve months to show that her plan would work; otherwise she needed to come back to the convent.

On August 16, 1948, Sister Teresa quietly slipped out of the convent. No one saw her go. And instead of wearing the clothes of her order, she was dressed in a blue and white Indian sari with a simple cross on her left shoulder. That was the day she looked into the compass of her heart and found the needle pointing a new direction. She chose to work in Motijhil, a slum of slums. She worked alone at first. She had no money, but began a school—and until some supplies were donated she simply taught by writing in the dirt.

Sister Teresa knew her mission; she planned her life journey. Her goal: to help others. She is the ultimate example of the Power of One. One woman who touched numerous lives—and left a legacy far larger, for Sister Teresa is the one who founded the Missionaries of Charity.

Eventually other people joined her on her journey—individuals making a difference. She soon became known as Mother Teresa.

Mother Teresa worked most of her life in the heat, filth, and misery of Calcutta. She was persistent; she wanted to help the poor and the terminally ill. She could have allowed the difficulties to stand in her way—or her selfishness to lead her to a better life.

But her faith and love of people who couldn't help themselves spurred her to continue. Alone, she couldn't save every person. Far from it. But her perseverance did touch the lives of many. And her example motivated far more people to follow in her footsteps.

Mother Teresa knew that she would never be repaid for her time and effort, at least not in a monetary way. But she probably wouldn't have accepted the money even if the people she helped could have paid. Instead, she did it for the reward of helping others, for the love she gave and for the love she got in return.

In our culture, it's not common to do something without expecting a favor in return. The phrase "there's no such thing as a free lunch" is synonymous with America, at least for most. But it doesn't have to be that way.

There are intangible rewards in following the Power of One: satisfaction of a job well done, a strong reputation, improving the lives of others, being loved and trusted, and so much more. Mother Teresa used the guidance system of the Power of One to take her to the finish line. And what a life well spent!

SUMMARIZING PRINCIPLES

1. Much of the journey requires us to glance down and find our bearings and direction.

2. We need a moral compass to help navigate the moments when we feel lost and uncertain.

3. We all have the ability to build a moral GPS (global positioning system) in our hearts and conscience.

4. Many decisions in life are more heart decisions than head decisions.

MAKING EVALUATION

I remember the very first time I used a GPS. I had flown into Washington, D.C., and had very little time to spare. The rental car company I normally used was out of cars, so I moved up and down the counter looking for anyone who had an unclaimed vehicle. Alas, one car was left. But it was going to be more expensive because it had this new contraption called a Magellan Never Lost system.

I thought to myself, *This could really work out well. Washington, D.C., is one of those cities that I find enormously confusing to drive in. I'm normally very good with directions and road sense, but D.C. just turns me around.*

I had four back-to-back meetings spread out all over the city. But no fear, I had the smooth-talking electronic-gadget guide telling me exactly when to turn, merge or redirect. No thinking, just steering. Magellan was doing all the brain work.

What would it be like to have a moral GPS unit? Let's call it a Golden Compass of sorts. It could evaluate our current ethical position and provide direction for us to get to our goal of the good, the right, and the true. The Power of One is the moral compass. It can give us all the direction and guidance we need for the journey.

Why do we need a Moral GPS? Check out the following benefits of the Golden Compass:

> *Efforts and courage are not enough without purpose and direction.*
>
> —JOHN F. KENNEDY

We find ourselves lost.

We look up and things don't look familiar anymore. We're no longer in the world of black-and-white behavior, but somewhere in that shadowy gray area of ethical choices. When we're lost in the depths of subjectivity and rationalization, the Golden Compass can give us an objective point of view, showing our placement in the situation and our true motivation for the actions we're planning to take. Knowing this information helps us make clearer decisions.

We get confused and overwhelmed.

Many times we are thrust into situations that overwhelm us. When he was sentenced to jail for the Watergate scandal, Jeb Stuart Magruder said, "Somewhere between my ambition and my ideals, I lost my ethical compass. I found myself on a path that had not been intended for me by my parents or by my principles or by my own ethical instincts. It has led me to this courtroom." Magruder, as well as many of us, would be well served to pull out the Golden Compass in times like this.

We get stuck in the ditch.

None of us are immune from falling in a ditch and needing a boost to get out. As a matter of fact, we all fall sometime, somewhere. The big question will then be, will you stay in the ditch and sink deeper or do you regroup, reset your coordinates, and climb back in the race? With a Golden Compass, you'll get going again a lot quicker—and back on the right track too.

We forget our original plan and get distracted.

A good start sometimes gets sidetracked. Many times we start very clear, but somewhere along the journey we lose our lighthouse. It's not enough just to start the good fight; you must end the good fight well too.

We need to know what is true, right, and good.

Many times an ethical decision comes down to doing the right thing regardless of the cost. The Golden Compass helps us clearly see the right thing to do. Let's face it, we live in a relativistic society. Truth is sometimes hazy. Even someone desiring to do the right thing may have trouble determining what the right thing truly is! The Golden Compass always points to the truth. Our job is to follow its direction.

Knowing where you are and where you need to go often isn't enough. You also need to know how to get there. The Golden Compass acts as a guide to get us to our destination. As we navigate the world of ethical choices, we have a consistent direction to choose to treat others as we want to be treated. These directions lead us home every time. But we have to make sure our compass works first.

For example, in the Disney movie *Pirates of the Caribbean*, Captain Jack Sparrow is the bad pirate who turns out to be a helpful mate once the movie takes sail. He shows up with a pistol carrying only one bullet, an antique triangle leather hat, and a compass that doesn't work.

An early scene shows a member of the British Royal Navy looking over Sparrow's paltry assembly of worldly goods and starts the humorous development of the captain's swagger. He says, looking down his nose, to Jack, "What kind of captain has a compass that doesn't even work?" And then the line appears that goes throughout the movie, "You are undoubtedly the worst pirate I have ever seen." That line is repeated until the end of the movie when Captain Jack has his compass out, skillfully navigating the *Black Pearl* through treacherous shark-infested, ship-carcass-filled waters. It is written into the scene the obvious assumption that typical navigational instruments are not enough to guide a ship through the cove Captain Jack is creeping through. It is hard to see that scene without flashbacks of the repeated line "You are undoubtedly the worst pirate I have ever seen."

Leaders must have an ethical compass. They must be able to steer their lives and the lives of those around them through the dangerous rocks.

A friend and I just spent the lunch hour talking through a big decision. He had one of the

> *People, like nails, lose their effectiveness when they lose direction and begin to bend.*
>
> —WALTER SAVAGE LANDOR

biggest decisions of his career to make. At the end of the lunch he said, "This is more about a decision of the heart than a decision of the head." I need an extraordinary guidance system to navigate this decision. The Golden Compass can be that kind of instrument.

1. Do you have an internal moral compass that can help you when your decision has to be ruled from the heart, not just the head?

_____

_____

2. Why are ethical decisions sometimes a little hazy?

_____

_____

TAKING ACTION

1. Have you ever needed guidance and direction because of these situations?
   - *We find ourselves lost.*
   - *We get confused and overwhelmed.*
   - *We get stuck in the ditch.*
   - *We forget our original plan and path and get distracted.*
   - *We need to know what is true, right, and good.*

2. What do you traditionally use to help you navigate your journey?

_____

_____

Every compass is designed to point north. The value of the compass hinges on the consistency of it pointing to the north!

The golden rule acts as that Moral North. It is a consistent landmark to guide us and give us our bearings. While attending graduate school, I commuted to Dallas, Texas, for my classes. The school was located between the Baylor Medical Center and an old, windowless, brown office tower owned by a telecommunications company. Each building was more than twenty stories tall and formed a towering presence in the neighborhood. Downtown Dallas could be seen in the distance, but was still a few miles away. The school was nestled in between these two buildings and surrounded by a several blocks of one-story houses, businesses, and fast-food restaurants.

While attending classes for several years, I would journey out into the nearby community to eat, shop, or meet someone for an appointment. The neighborhood was a combination of one-way streets and contained a couple of streets that reversed directions in a few lanes in the morning and evening to accommodate the commuters. Needless to say, I found myself confused on several occasions during my time in school.

I figured out pretty quickly that whenever I got lost, all I needed to do was look for my two buildings. After finding the Baylor Medical Center and the brown, windowless telecommunications building, I simply drove toward them. It was a great plan because I could always see them towering over the neighborhood. They never moved. Time and time again they proved faithful to me.

How we need such an ethical landmark today. The Golden Compass is designed to consistently lead us to what is good, right, and true, by using the golden rule as its "true north." The golden rule is our landmark. It stands firm as a tested and accepted beacon, pointing the way to ethical success. So when the circumstance of ethical fog blinds us, we go for our Golden Compass and ask, "How would I like to be treated in this situation?"

Why is the golden rule a landmark to guide us?

- *It is unchanging.* No matter what the situation, treating someone the way you would want to be treated is steady.
- *It is universal.* No matter when, where, or what, all people want to be treated right.
- *It is objective.* Treating others as you want to be treated is an objective test of our motives and actions.

How has the golden rule helped you make a decision when you were cloudy, confused, or just plain ol' lost?

You have riches and freedom here but I feel no sense of faith or direction. —Lech Walesa

---

Day 11

THE GOLDEN ZONE

If we had only one rule in this company, it would be the Golden Rule. If we've got that one right, no other rules are necessary.

—JIM BLANCHARD CEO, SYNOVUS FINANCIAL CORP.

DRIVING THOUGHT

The Power of One is the booster vitamin for relationships, the sweet spot for personal ambition, and the strike zone for individual achievement.

DRILLING DOWN

Jim Blanchard is the CEO of Synovus Financial Corp., a holding company for thirty-eight banks in five states, and 80 percent owner of an electronic payment services provider (called TSYS). The company's Web site states that its name is "a combination of the words *synergy* and *novus*—*synergy*, meaning the interaction of separate components such that the result is greater than the sum of its parts; and *novus*, which means usually of superior quality and different from the others listed in the same category." The organization possesses more than $18 billion in assets, employs more than nine thousand people, and is a component of the Standard & Poor's 500 index (NYSE: SNV).[1]

If you keep up with business news, you may have heard of Synovus. In 1998, *Fortune* magazine began publishing its list of the 100 Best Companies to Work For in America. In 1999, Synovus was ranked number one! The company has been on that list every year since its inception. (The list that came out in January of 2003 ranked Synovus ninth in the nation.)

As a business owner, I wanted to find out how one went about creating the best company to work for in the United States. So I talked to Jim. He told me that a few years after graduating from law school in 1965, at age twenty-nine he was selected to head the Columbus Bank and Trust Company. Over the years he built and expanded the business. But then in the 1990s, he realized that he wanted to make sure the principles and values he had always used personally to conduct business would become part of the culture of the organization. "We needed to institutionalize it, and we needed to enforce it and reinforce it," he said. And that meant making changes—big changes. Many policies were dismantled that had developed over the years, such as the promotion system, salary administration, and the review process.

They also initiated what Jim calls a People Development Component, the core of which is a commitment to their workforce. Jim explained,

> As leaders of Synovus, we said we were not going to allow a mean-spirited, manipulative, commanding sort of leadership to exist in this company any longer. And we were going to remediate anybody who was like that—if they were willing to try. But if they couldn't or wouldn't change, then we would ask them to go somewhere else.
>
> This is going to be a safe place to work. Employees are not going to be harassed. They are not going to be jerked around—we call that "salute the flag and kick the dog," meaning you say all the right things, but then you go back to your office and just beat up the folks. I stood up in a number of forums and said, "I'm writing you a blank check on this promise, and I want you to present it for payment. And if the check bounces, then you've got no reason to believe anything I tell you ever again."
>
> Very quickly the light of day shone on the bad leaders. We've had two to three hundred of them transition out in the last six or eight years, because they wouldn't live up to the standard of treating folks right, with respect, admiration, appreciation, consideration. And basically we culminated all of this by saying that if we had only one rule in this company, it would be the golden rule. If we've got that one right, no other rules are necessary.[2]

SUMMARIZING PRINCIPLES

1. The Golden Zone is a visible slice of life when someone is doing the good, the right, and the true with rhythm and regularity.

2. The Golden Zone is where everyone seeks to be and do their best. It is the place where young emerging players want to stay, and seasoned veterans don't want to leave.

MAKING EVALUATION

The Power of One is the booster vitamin for relationships, the sweet spot for personal ambition, and the strike zone for individual achievement.

For the last three years I have had the chance to take my son to a place called Lost Valley Ranch. It is a five-star dude ranch that sits in a valley surrounded by three sides of a national forest. I was invited to speak to a group of businessmen from Denver and Colorado Springs. It has become such a highlight for us. The first year we started a tradition that we have looked forward to each passing year. It was riding our horses at full gallop in the snow down untouched trails of white powder as deep as the horse could possibly run through.

Then something happened that changed everything. A fire burned the forest surrounding the ranch. You might remember hearing about the Colorado forest fires. The ranch itself was spared. A small strip of green grass and a few lodges are all that survived. But everything else was scarred and black. I had prepared my son for what he would see. As we rode through, there were still patches of snow, but the sight was completely different.

The head wrangler, who is a close friend of our family, told us there was a burn zone that simply rode with the wind and destroyed everything in its path. Trees hundreds of years old were brought to the ground as a result of the fires.

> *Make good habits and they will make you.*
>
> —PARKS COUSINS

The burn zone was sobering. Later that evening we watched a video clip that the Forest Service had prepared on the fire. Watching that video was sobering. There could not be a more striking opposite to use in thinking of the Golden Zone. The Golden Zone is a visible slice of life when someone is doing the good, the right, and the true with rhythm and regularity. Unlike the forest fire, the harvest of such a life is constant growth, life, and health. It is simply the zone when there is an ethical momentum.

Doing right can be addictive. We always hear of bad addictions, but doing good in life can also be an addiction—and a healthy addiction. Behaving ethically develops a sense of moral rhythm in our lives.

Have you seen the movie *The Sandlot?* It's the early 1960s, and fifth grader Scotty Smalls has just moved into town with his folks. Kids call him a dork—he can't even throw a baseball. But all that changes when Bennie Rodriguez, the leader of the neighborhood gang, recruits Smalls to play ball on his sandlot team. It's the beginning of a magical summer of baseball. Smalls's first day on the sandlot is awkward at best.

Halfway through practice, Rodriguez calls Scotty in from the outfield. He sees something in Smalls the other guys on the team fail to see—a desire to learn, a love to play. After receiving some tips on how to throw a baseball the same way you throw a newspaper, Smalls wants to know how to catch a ball. Rodriguez coaches Smalls to hold his glove open above his head and assures him, "It'll do the rest."

Once everyone is in position, Rodriguez steps to the plate with bat and ball in hand. Confident that he can strategically hit the ball in close proximity to Smalls's glove, he calls to the rookie center fielder, "Smalls, throw it to second." He hits a precisely placed fly ball to center. There

Smalls stands with glove in the air, eyes closed, whispering, "Please catch it, please catch it, please catch it . . ." The catch is made. The team is astonished. The throw is completed to second and Rodriguez and Smalls have just found The Golden Zone.

The Golden Zone is where everyone seeks to be and do their best. It is the place where it is more about "we" than "me." It is the place where young emerging players want to stay, and seasoned veterans don't want to leave.

What makes the zone golden is the application of the golden rule. We enter the zone when we treat others as we would want to be treated. Bennie Rodriguez applies it on a sandlot; Jim Blanchard applies it in a holding company. The net effect is the same: optimum performance and maximum growth.

> *Treat people as if they were what they ought to be and you helped them become what they are capable of being.*
>
> —GOETHE

How do you transform your business, your home, or the Little League team you coach, into a Golden Zone?

It starts with a little recognition . . .

Recognize It Is Not About You

Your personal desires and achievements are not the end goal. How your achievements are made and how you treat others are a big measure of success. At the heart of living right is recognizing that we are not the center of the universe. The world does not revolve around us. We enter the Golden Zone when we live to see others succeed in life.

Recognize That All People, Regardless of Position or Role, Deserve to Be Treated Well

Often we have no problem treating well those who can add benefit to our lives. Sometimes we tend to treat those below us in rank, financial status, or importance as second-class citizens. We enter the Golden Zone when we treat everyone with dignity, regardless of their impact on us or our desired outcomes.

Recognize That Helping Others Win Is a Win for You

The Golden Zone takes us to a different level of success. Succeeding on your own is one thing, but enabling others to succeed is off the charts. As a manager or coworker, we are in the Golden Zone when we find joy and fulfillment in helping others succeed.

1. Can you identify someone in your life story that has affected your success through inspiration, teaching, or modeling? Who? How did he or she do this?

2. What was this person's main mode of impact?

TAKING ACTION

In the movie *The Sandlot*, Rodriguez provides some insight into six key concepts that make the transformation possible.

- Have a contagious passion for the game.
- Champion the strengths of the team.
- Compensate for weaknesses.
- Allow the freedom to fail.
- Keep the learning curve high.
- Have fun!

1. If you were going to outline the common elements of all Golden Zones, what would they have?

_____

_____

_____

2. Do you know anyone who lives life in the Golden Zone? Can you name three?

_____

_____

_____

3. Does your ethical track record look more like a destructive Burn Zone than it does the Golden Zone?

_____

A candle loses nothing of its light by lighting another candle.
—Spurgeon

Day 12

I Want to Be Valued

Never miss an opportunity to praise someone in public.

—Bob Briner

Driving Thought

The Power of One means that I make others feel important—and I genuinely believe in their value.

Drilling Down

Wilbur "Shooter" Flatch can still taste it on his lips. The glory was almost his. The victory was almost his as well. The game was the Indiana State Sectionals.

Picture the scene: a game-winning shot. But it bounces off the rim, and "Shooter" loses the game. He was devastated—and still is.

Shooter is a former high-school basketball great; he's now a wounded head of a broken home and the father of a disappointed son. The only taste on his lips these days is alcohol, and lots of it. He went from town hero to town drunk in such a few short years. Often in his drunken binges, he relives the shot that brought disappointment, pain, and shattered confidence.

Then comes Norman Dale to coach the team at Shooter's alma mater. Shooter's son is on the team. The story unfolds in David Anspaugh's 1986 film *Hoosiers*, a movie about the real value and worth of individuals and about big comebacks.

Coach Dale sees within Shooter something Shooter has forgotten. He sees *value*. Dale knows that Shooter still understands basketball's finer points, and he enables Shooter to find his way out of the bottle long enough to regain his self-respect.

It all begins when Dale brings Shooter on board as an assistant coach. One night, in front of the home crowd, Dale purposefully has himself ejected from the game in order to hand Shooter the coaching job for the evening. But what Shooter didn't realize was that Dale was handing him much more than a job. He was giving him a taste of glory and victory, and much more importantly he was giving him self-worth and value he never thought possible.

Shooter's comeback wasn't without failure. He had a chance to shine, but he "dropped the ball," so to speak. But because of Dale's influence, the recovery didn't take quite as long as the first time. The story ends with Shooter still vulnerable, but with a taste of hope and victory on his lips as he repairs his relationship with his son.

The Power of One means that I make others feel important—and I genuinely believe in their value. Do you believe in the value of others? And do you take the time and effort to tell people you believe in them? That's the crucial step that many of us are missing in our relationships with others.

SUMMARIZING PRINCIPLES

1. Deep down, all people want to feel that they are an asset, rather than a liability, to the organization, team, family, or group to which they belong.

2. Invest in human capital at personal expense.

3. Valuing others is the foundation of the golden rule.

MAKING EVALUATION

Have you ever been made to feel worthless by another person? Perhaps a boss, a competitor, a parent, or a spouse told you that you had nothing to offer. Or perhaps you've been publicly humiliated. If so, then you know how important it is to be valued by another human being. Encouragement really is oxygen to the soul!

As a parent, we desire to see our children feel valued and filled with confidence about who they are. Unfortunately, not everyone they come in contact with has the same plan. I remember one day when my son went out to join some older neighborhood kids who were playing outside. As I watched through the window, he approached them, and I could tell he was asking these boys, who were older than him, if he could play. In his innocence he had yet to realize that older boys don't value younger kids during neighborhood playtime. The boys harshly told him that he couldn't play with them and then ran off as fast as they could so he couldn't catch them.

> *I have yet to find a man, whatever his situation in life, who did not do better work and put forth more effort under a spirit of approval than he ever would do under a spirit of criticism.*
>
> — CHARLES SCHWAB

You could see the disappointment in him through his physical posture. His shoulders slumped, his head hung low, and he dragged his feet as he walked back to our yard and sat down. He sat there staring at the street, elbows on his knees, his cheeks buried in his hands, and tears rolling down his face. It was pitiful. He felt no value. Luckily good ol' dad was there to show him that he is the most valued kid in the neighborhood!

Mary Kay Ash, the founder of her own beauty products line, understood the importance of making people understand their value. She once said, *"Everyone has an invisible sign saying, 'Make me feel important.' Never forget this message when dealing with people of all ages."* Do you make others feel valued?

1. Have you ever felt unvalued, or rejected, by another person?

_____

_____

_____

2. How does being unvalued change your view of the other person?

_____

_____

_____

3. How does being unvalued change how you interact with that person?

_____

_____

_____

4. How does being unvalued affect your performance? Your mood?

_____

_____

_____

Go back with me to the same neighborhood and the same son that we talked about earlier. But this time let's hear a different kind of story. Before he bought a gas scooter, my son loved to ride his bike. For Christmas one year, Santa brought him a really sharp bike with dual hand brakes, flame stickers, and knobby dirt tires. He rode it so much that he wore the training wheels off of their rims. He wanted desperately to ride the bike, but the training wheels were toast. I challenged him to learn to ride without them. Even though it was a little premature for his age and skill level, I knew he could do it.

So we began the process one Saturday afternoon. After an hour of letting go and reattaching myself to him, he began to catch on to the balance needed to ride the bike. I remember his first successful twenty-yard solo ride. He was so proud and wanted to try again. I noticed a few neighbors milling around their yards that afternoon. I whispered to my son to show them his newly found skill of riding solo. He yelled to them all, "Hey, watch this! I can ride by myself without my training wheels." I gave him a shove and he took off for about a fifty-yard run.

The neighbors applauded and encouraged him. "Way to go!" "That's great!" "You sure are a fast learner!" His face was beaming. I added my approval. He felt confident. He felt proud. You could see it in the way he walked, and in the tone of his voice. He was feeling valuable. Isn't it amazing how a few words or actions of encouragement can change a person's perspective?

If you were to write down all the possible ways to motivate people to do better work, friendly praise would have to come near the head of your list.

—HANNAH WHITALL SMITH

The most amazing thing is that we could be talking about middle-aged men and women in their corporate neighborhood at the same time. Instead of playing games and riding bikes, it is giving presentations, getting the business, and things of that sort. But the core idea doesn't change one shred. We all have an invisible sign that says, "Make me feel valued and important."

1. Can you think of a time when a person offered you some timely encouragement that really affected your life?

_____

_____

_____

2. How does feeling valued affect our view of ourselves?

_____

_____

_____

3. How does feeling valued affect our performance?

_____

_____

_____

4. How do we view those who are encouraging to us?

_____

_____

_____

TAKING ACTION

There is no doubt that we all want to feel valued by others and by the organizations in which we belong. Deep down all people want to feel that they matter—and they do, because they have dignity as human beings. We exert the Power of One when we intentionally act in a manner that seeks to add high amounts of value to others. For instance, a coach has the opportunity to not only teach his or her sport or make game decisions for the team, he or she also has the opportunity to add high amounts of value to each player through encouraging them and believing in them. A manager not only can regulate performance, assign tasks, and teach skills, but can also add high value through inspiration, appreciation, and encouragement.

Consider the following High-Value steps:

High-Value Thinking

Did you know that in the American marketplace today, 70 percent of the people who leave their jobs do so because they don't feel valued? That's an indictment of how poorly many business-people treat their employees. There isn't a person in the world who doesn't want to be valued by others. Don't you want others to accept you for who you are and show you through their actions that you matter?

1. You are a manager. Your job is to efficiently mobilize the company workforce to get results. You can choose your management style. Why would managing in a way that builds value in your employees be better than good old-fashioned intimidation and fear?

_____

_____

_____

2. How could making your employees feel valued increase productivity?

_____

_____

_____

High-Value Expression

Invest in human capital at personal expense this month. Author Gary Chapman has identified five love languages that people speak. In essence, they represent how we express and
receive value and worth from one another. The five languages:

- **Words of Affirmation** is using words to affirm the other person. It is a key way to
  express value. Hallmark makes a lot of money each year selling words of
  encouragement.

- **Quality Time** is giving someone your undivided attention. The important thing is
  not the activity but that you have time together. When you express value through
  quality time, you give a person a part of your life.

- **Gift Giving** is a universal expression of value and worth. Gifts need not be
  expensive.

- **Acts of Service** is the golden rule in action. Doing something that you know the
  other person would like communicates volumes. The person who speaks this
  language is always looking for things he can do for others, and is greatly honored
  when you do things for him.

- **Physical Touch,** such as a pat on the back, an elbow at the appropriate moment, a
  firm handshake, a hug, a back scratch, a foot massage, carries great power. The
  person who speaks this language expresses and receives value through touch.

1. What is your primary language?

_____

_____

2. Think of the top five relationships you have at work. Identify the language of each
   person. How could you change the way you interact with each person based on this
   information?

Name	Language
1. _____	_____
2. _____	_____
3. _____	_____
4. _____	_____
5. _____	_____

High-Value Action

Add value to those around you this week. Whether at home, the office, or in the community, take some steps to build up those in your sphere of influence.

Write a note.

Express how much you value someone through a handwritten note. Believe it or not, that person may tuck it away and look at it for years.

Share a compliment.

Add value to someone by telling her that she is really good at something. Express admiration for a skill or quality she possesses.

Catch someone doing something right.

We are really good at reminding people when they have let us down. Spend some time appreciating people for the little things they do right every day. We often take these for granted.

Express some interest.

Ask people how they are doing and listen to their answers. Show that you care about them and the things in their lives that aren't related to what you need from them.

Brag on someone in front of others.

It is great to receive a compliment from someone. It is far greater for someone else to hear you getting that compliment!

Give a gift.

Show you value someone by spending some of your money on him. We all love to receive a little something from another person.

The deepest craving in human nature is the craving to be appreciated. —William James

---

Day 13

I Want to Be Trusted

Trust is the central issue in human relationships within and outside organizations. Without trust you cannot lead. Without trust you cannot get extraordinary things done.

—Kouzes and Posner

Driving Thought

The Power of One means that I give others the benefit of the doubt and choose to believe in their goodness.

Drilling Down

Trust in others doesn't come easily these days. In a world of corporate scandal, rampant layoffs, and company disloyalty, executives and employees alike would have no reason to trust one another. But James Granger, a new CEO, chose to put trust in his employees—against the wishes of his fellow executives.

Granger stepped into the job of CEO of Norstan Inc., a communications technology company targeting the enterprise market in North America in 2000. The company was a mess. An interim executive team allowed the company's values-based philosophy to languish. The company was losing $8 million per quarter, had $80 million in debt, and was within days of filing bankruptcy.

By all views, the company situation looked dismal. Why Granger chose to share the company's dire financial straits with employees, no one could understand. But Granger wanted to give his employees the benefit of the doubt. He chose to be forthright with his employees about the true financial picture.

He obviously knew what he was doing. He trusted that his employees would take the information as motivation to do better, work harder, and bring about a company turnaround. And it worked. His honesty encouraged employees to think creatively and find ways to help turn the company around.

They understood when Granger had to delay raises for a quarter. And by being honest with his vendors, he was able to procure similar delays in payments. By the first quarter of 2001, profitability had returned; Granger and his devoted team had reduced their debt to nearly nothing. As a result, stock value improved.[1]

Granger could have handled the situation much differently. He could have kept information from staff members—even fired a bunch of them in order to save money. He wouldn't have been out of line in doing so, because that's how many companies work. But he was practicing the Power of One—an understanding of the golden rule—that made him think more of his employees.

He expected they would not quit upon hearing the bad news—they probably suspected it anyway. And he chose to believe that instead of leaving the company or revolting, they would pitch in to save the company. And *because* he chose to believe this about his employees, they proved him right.

Showing people you have faith in them often makes them work even harder to prove you right. If you don't trust them, they won't have any reason to work hard for you. It's your call; which will it be?

> *If you mistrust your employees you will be right 3 percent of the time. If you trust people until they give you a reason not to, you will be right 97 percent of the time.*
>
> —Wolf J. Rinke

SUMMARIZING PRINCIPLES

1. People deserve to be trusted until they have proven repeatedly that they cannot be trusted.

2. Trusting others is good for them and good for us.

3. Trust is the foundation of all good relationships.

4. The greater the degree of sustained integrity that is displayed in an individual, the easier it is to trust him or her.

5. Mistrust acts as a cancer that spreads uncontrollably.

MAKING EVALUATION

Knowing that what you do matters builds your self-confidence and self-worth. The people who work with you and for you possess the same desire—even those who don't show it.

Human relations expert and author Donald Laird asserted, "Always help people increase their own self-esteem. Develop your skill in making other people feel important. There is hardly a higher compliment you can pay an individual than helping him to be useful and to find satisfaction in his usefulness."

How can you do that? Begin by letting people know that you appreciate their efforts. Thank them at every opportunity. Give credit to others every time you can. And make it a point to praise people in the presence of those closest to them, such as family members.

Trust lies at the heart of all high-performing organizations. In his book *The Five Dysfunctions of a Team*, Patrick Lencioni states that the number-one dysfunction of leadership in teams is an absence of trust. In the absence of trust, Lencioni says people:

> *Faith is not belief without proof, but trust without reservation.*
> —ELTON TRUEBLOOD

- conceal weaknesses and mistakes from one another
- hesitate to ask for help or provide constructive feedback
- hesitate to offer outside their own area of responsibility
- jump to conclusions about the intentions and aptitudes of others without attempting to clarify them
- fail to recognize and tap into one another's skills and experiences
- waste time and energy managing their behaviors for effect
- hold grudges
- dread meetings and find reason to avoid spending time together[2]

We all deeply desire to be trusted. Without trust there can be no relationship. Trust is the foundation of all good relationships. If you don't have trust, there can be no open and honest interaction, and the relationship will only be temporary. In order to have trust in someone or be trusted, we have to act in a trustworthy manner. The greater the degree of sustained integrity that is displayed in an individual, the easier it is to trust him or her.

Are You Trustworthy?

Check out the following list of trust-breaking behaviors. Grade yourself in trustworthiness by circling the most appropriate evaluation point following each statement:

1. I fail to keep my time commitments

      Never   **Sometimes**   **Frequently**   **Always**

2. I fail to accomplish the tasks I am responsible for

      Never   **Sometimes**   **Frequently**   **Always**

3. I use lies to prevent tense moments

      Never   **Sometimes**   **Frequently**   **Always**

4. I share confidential conversations with other people

      Never   **Sometimes**   **Frequently**   **Always**

5. I borrow something and fail to return it to the proper location in a timely manner

      Never   **Sometimes**   **Frequently**   **Always**

6. I talk about someone maliciously behind his/her back

      Never   **Sometimes**   **Frequently**   **Always**

7. I gossip about others

      Never   **Sometimes**   **Frequently**   **Always**

8. I steal from others

      Never   **Sometimes**   **Frequently**   **Always**

9. I break the operating rules of my organization

      Never   **Sometimes**   **Frequently**   **Always**

10. I fail to keep my financial obligations fully and on time

      Never   **Sometimes**   **Frequently**   **Always**

11. I manipulate a situation or person to get what I want

      Never   **Sometimes**   **Frequently**   **Always**

12. I break a previous commitment because of a new opportunity

      Never   **Sometimes**   **Frequently**   **Always**

- Based on your answers to the questions above, are you a trustworthy person?

  Never **Sometimes** **Frequently** **Always**

- Name an area of concern in which you need to guard yourself.

  _____

  _____

  _____

- How can you begin to build greater trust from others?

  _____

  _____

  _____

- Which of the above trust breakers, if broken by one of your associates, would create the greatest amount of distrust in you? Why?

  _____

  _____

  _____

TAKING ACTION

A friend recounted a story as we were discussing the topic of trust. He said it was one of the earliest gifts of someone else's trust in him that he can remember. To this day, twenty-five years later, it still is a tattoo on his heart regarding the enormous value of giving away trust. Here's his story:

"Growing up in Memphis, Tennessee I had little freedom. Our fair city offered us many opportunities for entertainment and life experience, but it offered no assurance of safety to my parents. As an eight-year-old boy with a bike, I had about a three-hundred-yard radius in which I could move about freely in our neighborhood. This enabled me to ride down about two different streets that intersected ours. It wasn't that my parents didn't trust me, although I am sure my lack of maturity figured into it; the matter was that they did not trust the environment. Too many cars, too many people they didn't know.

"When we eventually moved to a small town in which my mother had grown up, things changed significantly. It wasn't Mayberry, but it was pretty close. I was shocked when I asked my father if I could ride my bike to a friend's birthday party one Saturday. He asked me whether I knew the way, and then granted permission! I was invigorated. He trusted me to stay out of trouble, to navigate my way, to act responsibly. I couldn't wait to see the look on my friends' faces when I rolled up on my bike, having traveled a mile and a half on my own.

"However, a problem developed when I found myself lost on my way to the party. I got my directions mixed up and wandered the town for more than an hour. Eventually, I recognized the church down the street from my grandmother's house and rode rapidly to her home, where I broke down tearfully on her front porch. She was very sympathetic to my scenario. She offered a hug, a piece of candy, and a ride home. She even expressed shock that I had been given freedom to venture out such a long distance on my own. I can remember her clearly communicating that to my father when she drove me home and delivered me, tearstained, without ever having arrived at the party.

> *Few things help an individual more than to place responsibility upon him, and to let him know that you trust him.*
>
> — BOOKER T. WASHINGTON

"Even though her rescue efforts and polite rebuke of my father's misplaced trust created a bit of tension at home that night, and even though I experienced the terror of being lost, and even though I missed a grand birthday party, I cherished the opportunity to be trusted. I relished in the fact that my father gave me a chance. He allowed me a shot at third-grade glory. I discovered then that trust is an empowering currency."

As my friend's story illustrates, we all desire for others to trust us, even at an early age. The golden rule challenges us to give our trust to others. While you cannot control whether people give you their trust, you can control your actions with them. And you can determine to give them *your* trust.

Former U.S. Secretary of State Henry L. Stimson remarked, "The chief lesson I have learned in a long life is that the only way you can make a man trustworthy is by trusting him; and the surest way to make him untrustworthy is to distrust him and show your distrust."

REACT

Interact with the following statements and examples. Do you agree or disagree? Write a brief thought in reaction.

- Trust from your superiors or company can enhance your performance. *For example: Your boss gives you the lead role in a sales pitch for a big client. You develop a greater sense of ownership and go the extra mile in preparation.*

    Agree / Disagree

    Thought?

    _____

    _____

    _____

    _____

    _____

- Trust should be given in proportion to trustworthy performance. *For example: The company probably shouldn't trust the pension fund to an associate who has mismanaged his expense account.*

    Agree / Disagree

    Thought?

    _____

    _____

    _____

    _____

    _____

- Trust should be hedged against the potential downfall. *For example: The company shouldn't put the cash-cow account in the hands of the new college intern.*

    Agree / Disagree

    Thought?

_____

_____

_____

_____

_____

- Trust should be able to be earned again after a failure. _For example: Outside of major moral failure, associates should be able to earn the company's trust after a setback through repeated trustworthy actions._

  Agree / Disagree

  Thought?

_____

_____

_____

_____

_____

- Trust is the key to developing others. _For example: A manager can only raise up his replacement by trusting him enough to give him the opportunity to perform managerial tasks. A salesman can only be developed by trusting him enough to give him an account._

  Agree / Disagree

  Thought?

_____

_____

_____

_____

- Trust allows the freedom to fail. *For example: A company leader entrusts a creative project to an employee who has less experience. Even with a great work ethic, the project fails. Yet the employee is given another project with pointers on how to improve.*

Agree / Disagree

Thought?

_____

_____

_____

_____

_____

It is more shameful to distrust our friends than to be deceived by them. —Francois De La Rochefoucauld

Day 14

I WANT TO BE RESPECTED

When someone prizes us just as we are, he or she confirms our existence.

—EUGENE KENNEDY

DRIVING THOUGHT

The Power of One means that I respect people, and sometimes need to take action that helps drive the level of respect up—for others and for myself.

DRILLING DOWN

Sometimes the simplest of actions carry the most profound of messages. Rosa Parks sent a message about racial segregation when she boarded a bus in Montgomery, Alabama, in December 1955, and sat down in row eleven. By law, the first ten rows of all buses in Montgomery were reserved for whites, and blacks were not allowed to sit in that section, even if the seats in that section were empty and blacks were standing in the aisle. If, however, the white section filled up, then the bus driver could ask the blacks to vacate seats in their section to make way for white folks. It was illegal for blacks to sit in the same twin seats with whites, or even across aisles from them.

On this winter evening close to Christmas, the back of the bus was full and then the front section also filled up. When white passengers were left standing, the bus driver ordered the blacks in the first row of the black section to vacate their seats. Three of the four did. Rosa Parks refused. The bus driver pulled over and called the police. The forty-two-year-old Parks was arrested and jailed. She was charged with violating the segregation laws of the state of Alabama.

Her refusal to be treated as less than fully human touched off the Montgomery bus boycott, and culminated in December of 1956 with a United States Supreme Court decision to outlaw racial segregation on public transportation.

Rosa Parks is a small woman with a huge legacy. Each and every time an interviewer came along to ask her questions, she responded with the same message over and over. "I simply wanted people to treat me with respect and basic human dignity. That is all." She stood up for what she thought was right—for herself and for others. In doing so, she helped drive up the respect for herself and for other black people in this divisive world.

SUMMARIZING PRINCIPLES

1. Most people greatly desire the respect of the people they work with.

2. Giving someone respect need not be overcomplicated or risky.

3. We all deserve a basic level of respect as members of the human race.

4. The respect employees receive gives them the freedom to perform at their best and the incentive to work with excellence.

MAKING EVALUATION

In 1967, Otis Redding wrote a #1 hit song for Aretha Franklin simply titled "Respect." In the song, Franklin literally spells out what she needs . . .

"R-E-S-P-E-C-T
Find out what it means to me
R-E-S-P-E-C-T
Take care, TCB."

We all want to be respected. And I'm not talking about the respect that comes from having the most experience, talent, age, or authority. By respect, I mean the common courtesy treatment that gives you dignity and confidence as a human being. When we lack respect for something or somebody, then we are more likely to neglect or mistreat that person or thing. We all deserve a basic level of respect as members of the human race. There is another level of respect or honor that is given to those we admire, but regardless of our ages, races, positions, or performance, we all deserve to be respected as a person.

In light of our desire to be treated with respect, the golden rule challenges us to give respect to others. Let's

> *Our early emphasis on human relations was not motivated by altruism but by the simple belief that if we respected our people and helped them respect themselves, the company would make the most profit.*
>
> —THOMAS J. WATSON JR.,
> IBM

follow Aretha Franklin's advice and begin to "take care of business" by working through the following:

No Respect

   Name five ways in which a person can show a lack of respect for you:

1. _____

2. _____

3. _____

4. _____

5. _____

How does being treated with a lack of respect make you feel? What kinds of emotions are stirred up inside of you when you are not respected?

_____

_____

_____

How do these disrespectful actions affect the way you interact with the offending party(s)?

_____

_____

_____

Are you guilty of any of the above-mentioned actions in your relationships? If yes, how have you shown a lack of respect?

_____

_____

_____

Respect

Name five ways in which a person can show respect for you:

1. _____
2. _____
3. _____
4. _____
5. _____

In what ways do these actions bring strength to your relationship with that person?

_____

_____

_____

Why is receiving respect so important?

_____

_____

_____

How do you regularly show respect in your relationships?

_____

_____

_____

Review the ten rules of respect previously mentioned in *There's No Such Thing As "Business" Ethics:*

1. If you have a problem with me, come to me (privately).
2. If I have a problem with you, I'll come to you (privately).
3. If someone has a problem with me and comes to you, send him or her to me. (I'll do the same for you.)
4. If someone consistently will not come to me, say, "Let's go see him together. I am sure he will see us about this." (I will do the same for you.)

5. Be careful how you interpret me; I'd rather do that. On matters that are unclear, do not feel pressured to interpret my feelings or thoughts. It is easy to misinterpret intentions.

6. I will be careful how I interpret you.

7. If it's confidential, don't tell. If you or anyone else comes to me in confidence, I won't tell unless (a) the person is going to harm himself/herself, (b) the person is going to physically harm someone else, (c) a child has been physically or sexually abused. I expect the same from you.

8. I do not read unsigned letters or notes.

9. I do not manipulate; I will not be manipulated; do not let others manipulate you. Do not let others try to manipulate me through you.

10. When in doubt, just say it. If I can answer it without misrepresenting something or breaking confidence, I will.

We all want respect. We all can give respect. It starts with a simple determination on our part to treat others the same way we would want them to treat us. If we will do that, then the respect meter will start rising everywhere.

TAKING ACTION

Infamous comedian Rodney Dangerfield coined the phrase "I get no respect" in his stage act. For years people have laughed at Rodney's inability to generate respect from anyone he comes in contact with. Check out the following one-liners from Rodney's Web site:

> *Men are respectable only as they respect.*
>
> —RALPH WALDO EMERSON

> When I was a kid I got no respect. The time I was lost on the beach and the cop helped me look for my parents I said, "Do you think we'll find them?" He said, "I don't know, kid, there's so many places they could hide."
>
> It was the same way in the army, no respect; they gave me a uniform that glowed in the dark.
>
> I tell ya I get no respect from anyone. I bought a cemetery plot. The guy said, "There goes the neighborhood."
>
> I don't get no respect. I joined Gambler's Anonymous. They gave me 2 to 1 odds I don't make it.
>
> I don't get no respect at all from my dog. Well, he keeps barking at the front door. He don't want to go out. He wants me to leave.

With my wife I get no respect. I took her to a drive-in movie. I spent the whole night try-ing to find out what car she was in.[1]

Whether it was his wife, his parents, or other people he interacted with, Dangerfield has made a living on sharing the variety of ways he has been disrespected. We communicate respect for others or a lack of respect for them in a variety of ways.

To check your respect level, complete the table on page 102 that deals with the fruits of our actions each day.

We often show differing levels of respect to others based on their relationships to us. We often respect our bosses more than our employees. We respect our spouses more than our children. We respect our grandparents more than our cousins. It seems that we have been trained to show more respect to those higher than us on the organizational chart and less respect to those below us.

Maybe this is true because there are no impending ramifications for disrespecting someone who has no authority over you. If a parent disrespects his child, the child cannot ground the parent or withhold his allowance. If that same parent disrespected his boss, then he might find himself without a job. We therefore tend to find less pressure or responsibility to show respect to those who are younger, less talented, less expe-rienced, or simply lower in rank than us.

It is interesting, though, that respect is valued most by these very people in our lives. It is expected of them to respect us as their leaders. The golden rule challenges us to show them the same in return. Most people greatly desire the respect of the people they work for. And when employers give it freely, it creates a very positive working environment. Not only will it enhance the esteem of the workforce; it will enhance performance as well. This is true in the workplace as well as the home and the neighborhood.

Play the role of company president for this scenario.

> *Man wishes to be confirmed in his being by man and wishes to have a presence in the being of another. Secretly and bashfully he watches for a yes which can come to him from one human person to another.*
> —MARTIN BUBER

1. How can you as the head of your organization show respect to your employees?

_____

_____

_____

Action	Taking this action shows respect by . . .	Not taking this action shows a lack of respect by . . .
Listening	Expressing interest in another's opinion	Not valuing what someone has to say
Being on time	Valuing the time of others, keeping your commitment	Wasting the time of others, failing to live up to your commitments, being inconsiderate of other's schedules
Returning calls/e-mail		
Using kind words and a kind tone		
Not interrupting		
Cleanliness in your designated area		
Keeping your word		
Politeness, saying please and thank you		
Asking permission to borrow something		
Avoiding gossip		
Knocking before entering		
Turning off cell phones during meetings		
Avoiding humor that is off-color/offensive		

2. Why is showing respect to those under your leadership especially important?

_____

_____

_____

3. Why is showing respect to your peers and to those above you easier?

_____

_____

_____

4. How can respecting those under your leadership enhance performance?

_____

_____

_____

_____

Probably no greater honor can come to any man than the respect of his colleagues. —Cary Grant

_____

Day 15

I WANT TO BE UNDERSTOOD

When dealing with others seek first to understand then to be understood.

—HANS KÜNG

DRIVING THOUGHT

The Power of One is built on quick forgiveness, quiet consideration, and the spirit of the second chance.

DRILLING DOWN

It seemed like just another day at the Ashland County Airport in Ashland, Ohio. Instructors for the flight school were buzzing about, preparing for lessons, when Ralph Danison walked in. The eighteen-year-old announced he was scheduled for a lesson. But he didn't wait for the instructor.

Danison got more than a flying lesson that day. He got a lesson in trust, understanding, and most of all, survival. And he got a second chance at life.

The young man had an employee help him move the plane out of the hangar—the employee thought the instructor was on his way. Danison took a seat in the cockpit—and took off on his own.

The reasons for his solo flight weren't clear to anyone involved that day, until the end. Apparently, Danison, who had been treated for depression and anxiety for nearly a year, had decided he didn't want to live. One day short of starting college, Danison couldn't take the pressure anymore. His father died when Danison was nine; his mother battled cancer twice. Life just wasn't going as expected.

During his solo flight, Danison radioed Christine Hoadley, a twenty-three-year-old who was flying that day to qualify as a solo pilot on a Cessna 172. Danison called "Mayday!" then asked Hoadley to tell his family he loved them.

Hoadley wasn't going to let him go that easily. She knew what those words meant; a former member of her aviation fraternity in college had committed suicide by crashing his plane.

He said those very same words. She understood what Danison was going through, what he intended to do.

Because she understood, she was able to—eventually, and with the help of others—talk him through the procedures of landing a plane. She got him safely on the ground after several attempts.[1] It was as if Christine had the words of Lewis Thomas posted on the screen as she worked: "*Society evolves this way, not by shouting each other down, but by the unique capacity of unique, individual human beings to comprehend each other.*"

What Danison did can't be excused. He was arrested for felony grand theft of an aircraft. The point, however, is that Danison's predicament could have been avoided with a little understanding of his situation. Had he been able to express his feelings—and had people hear him and understand him—he may not have been driven to such extremes.

Like most situations in life, we just want other people to hear us out—nod a bit, sympathize, empathize if possible. We don't need people to necessarily agree with us; that's too much to ask. But a little understanding goes a long way.

You can't just expect others to understand you all the time. Give something back to others; take time to listen, tap into their thoughts, and feel what they're feeling. You never know whose life you might save—including your own.

SUMMARIZING PRINCIPLES

1. Everyone always wants to be understood, all of the time.
2. The need for understanding drives many people to extreme behavior. Some act out in rash conduct while others retreat into a cocoon of mistrust and self-doubt.
3. Understanding means you see my perspective. It doesn't automatically mean that you agree with my perspective.
4. Understanding is akin to sympathy and empathy, but isn't the same thing.
5. Understanding others requires that I lay down my quick judgment, self-interest, preoccupation, and careless flippancy.

MAKING EVALUATION

When dealing with others, seek first to understand, then to be understood. That requires an attitude of flexibility and teachableness. Theologian Hans Küng observed, "Understanding someone properly involves learning from him, and learning from someone properly involves changing oneself." Understanding other people means extending yourself to them and meeting them on their level. You have to put the burden of making a connection on yourself, not on them.

It's also wise to remember the words of inventor Charles Kettering: "There is a great difference between knowing and understanding: You can know a lot about something and not really understand it." The same can be said about people.

The Power of One means that we are willing to work to be understood, and also devote energy to understanding others who may need understanding. Contrary to popular belief, being understood sometimes requires effort on my part. It might mean that I have to learn to communicate a little differently: Should I talk a little more? A little less? No surprise, understanding others always takes some calories from me.

To understand means to perceive or uncover the essential nature of something. In the case of the Power of One, it's getting your hands around another person's core thoughts and feelings. Get inside his head. Walk in her shoes. See life from his or her angle. Climbing into the skin of your audience is key to all good communication.

Ted Geisel spent years stepping into the skin of his audience. He was already successful as an author when he agreed to a challenge—and inadvertently stepped into controversy. Better known as Dr. Seuss, Geisel focused his unique talent on writing books for children. The books took readers on a fantastic exploration of language. The titles themselves, like *Horton Hears a Who!* and *If I Ran the Zoo*, made people chuckle, as well as making them curious. And kids loved reading these stories. Why? Because Ted understood the minds of kids.

> *The man who can put himself in the place of other men, who can understand the workings of their minds, need never worry about what the future has in store for him.*
>
> —OWEN D. YOUNG

In 1956 an article appeared in *Life* magazine—and is still referenced today—titled "Why Johnny Can't Read." The author of that article made the case that one of the primary reasons that children were experiencing difficulty in learning to read was that the books used to teach reading were boring and ineffective. The writer suggested that Dr. Seuss write a book designed to help kids learn how to read.[2]

Dr. Seuss accepted that challenge. The experts gave him a list of 250 words that represented the vocabulary children could understand. That list cramped Dr. Seuss's style, as he was used to ranging far and wide in his use of words, including making up his own. But he worked within the strict limitations. To cure a bout of writer's block, he took the first two words on the list that rhymed—and *The Cat in the Hat* was born. Geisel originally thought the project would take a few weeks. It ended up taking nine months.

The books were an overwhelming and overnight success—except with the very folks for whom he had created the reading instruction tool: the educational establishment. Teachers refused to use the book, and people even boycotted it. Geisel also received criticism for using his pen name "Dr." because he didn't have a Ph.D. In addition, educators felt that the book trivialized the soberness of the learning process: Learning was serious, and this book was too much fun.

But an astounding thing happened. The primary customer, the kids, loved his work and wouldn't let it die. Geisel sought to understand the world of the children: their minds, their imaginations, their issues, their creativity, and anything and everything that shapes the world of a child. In short, he said to himself, "I want to understand the child. I did not write this for adults but for kids."[3]

It took years for teachers to change their opinion, but *The Cat in the Hat,* and the additional twenty-one beginning reading books that Geisel authored over thirty years—such as *Green Eggs and Ham* and *Fox in Socks*—have become an integral part of the teaching landscape for children learning how to read books and love language.

Understanding others is not always easy. But all good understanding begins with someone taking the time to see life from the eyes of the other person. The Power of One is at work when you seek to understand another person.

1. Have you ever felt misunderstood? Describe the situation.

_____

_____

_____

_____

_____

_____

2. What feelings did you experience when you were misunderstood?

_____

_____

3. Why do you think we so easily misunderstand others or are misunderstood by others?

_____

_____

_____

4. Are you a good listener? What is your most likely response when someone speaks to you?
- Did you say something?
- Could you repeat that?
- Sounds like you said _____!
- I think I got what you said.
- I heard you loud and clear!

5. How does it make you feel when you know that another person desires to understand you?

_____

_____

_____

TAKING ACTION

In order to live the Power of One in the area of understanding, you must work through two issues: perspective and skill.

Perspective

Who are you? Where are you from? What do you believe? The answers to these questions make a huge difference in how we communicate to and receive communication from others. We perceive the world around us through a set of lenses that have been crafted by the history of our human experiences. Understanding ourselves and seeking to understand the perspective of others is vital to good communication, which leads to mutual understanding.

Fill out the following personal perspective survey:

> *I know you believe you understand what you think I said but . . . I am not sure you realize that what you heard is not what I meant.*

1. Where were you raised?

_____

_____

2. What type of accent do you have?

_____

3. What race or nationality are you?

_____

4. What religious background do you have?

_____

5. What was your home life like growing up?

_____

_____

6. What is your current family situation?

_____

_____

7. How is your self-image?

_____

_____

8. Are you a passive or aggressive person?

_____

_____

9. How old are you?

10. Are you male or female?

Now add these things (and many more) together and you can develop a grid through which you interpret the world around you. Now imagine that the person you are seeking to understand is communicating to you through a grid that has a completely different background! We can be quick to find fault with others when they don't conform to the patterns or standards we hold. But if we make the effort to get to know another person (as well as understand our own perspectives), we often discover that his or her way isn't the wrong way—it's just a different way.

Skill

We all want to be understood and should seek to understand those around us. Much of our ability to understand another person comes from our communication skills. Think through the following skills in seeking to better understand those around you.

The Skill of Listening

1. Give the person your full attention and allow him to finish what he's saying before responding.
2. Turn your brain and your body toward him.
3. Before you respond to him, repeat back what you heard him say to see whether you accurately received his message. Try something like this, "What I hear you saying is . . ." If you misunderstood him, then he can correct you before you respond.
4. Maintain eye contact and provide nonverbal signs that tell him you understand.

The Skill of Communicating

1. Clearly state what you want, need, and feel. Good communication is accurate and clear. Accuracy is better achieved if you stick with a first-person perspective.
2. Use statements that begin with "I." For example, "I feel as if no one around here listens to me." This is a true statement and is better received than "You never listen to me!"
3. Don't tell a person what she is thinking or begin with an accusation. Let her know what you're thinking and feeling from your perspective.

4. Always be polite and remember that your tone and nonverbal signals help determine how others understand you.

The Skill of Avoidance

1. Avoid jumping to a response before you hear the other person completely.

2. Avoid assuming there is an agenda or hidden motive behind another's communication.

3. Avoid getting defensive if a person says you've offended him or let him down.

4. Avoid a counterattack when being confronted.

5. Avoid thinking that a perspective different from your own is wrong.

6. Avoid thinking that everything has to be fixed—and that you have to do it. Just listen and communicate "I understand."

In order to really understand, we need to listen, not reply. We need to listen long and attentively. In order to help anybody to open his heart we have to give him time, asking only a few questions, as carefully as possible in order to help him better explain his experience. —Paul Tournier

---

Day 16

I Don't Want Others to Take Advantage of Me

I had had enough. I just wanted to be treated like a human being.

—Rosa Parks

Driving Thought

The Power of One means that I come to grips with the fact that others will treat me unfairly sometimes—but that won't deter me from the golden walk.

Drilling Down

The scene was rather dramatic. One man was standing on a bulldozer. Another man had just climbed over the fence and was now standing next to the big machine that towered over him. A huge crowd of thousands of workers was on strike.

Just two sentences marked what turned out to be one of the most decisive moments of Polish history. "Remember me," yelled Lech Walesa to the director of the Gdansk shipyard. Walesa was trying to persuade striking shipyard workers to go on strike a cold December day in 1970. "I gave ten years' work to this shipyard and then was fired. Well, I'm here to tell you we're not going to listen anymore to your lying promises," he said. There and then he decided that he was going to draw a line in the dirt on being taken advantage of.

Walesa, a former car mechanic and army corporal, was working as an electrician for the shipyard. One year

That you may retain your self-respect, it is better to displease the people by doing what you know is right, than to temporarily please them by doing what you know is wrong.

—William J. H. Boetcker

married, he found himself embroiled in an uproar with the shipyards. A day after his outburst, the other shipyards in Gdansk and Gdyknia joined the sit-down strike. Soon, more than five hundred factories followed suit.

Many companies and people strike each year; this strike, however, was the beginning of a full-scale showdown with Poland's Communist government. The solidarity strike had struck.

Life wasn't easy for Walesa and his wife. He was briefly detained. He lost his job in 1976 as a result of his activities as a shop steward. Temporary jobs—and his Power of One—got him through.

In 1978 he began organizing free non-Communist trade unions. The state security service kept him under surveillance—and detained him regularly.

Walesa was being mistreated, along with numerous other workers. But he didn't let the situation deter him from his golden walk. He prayed, and every evening in the Lenin Shipyard there was Mass, with thousands of workers on their knees, singing and praying. They knew they were doing the right thing in striking out for freedom—but it didn't make the circumstances any easier. Still, he persisted.

In 1980 he led the Gdansk shipyard strike, which opened the door for many more strikes throughout Poland. People saw Walesa as the leader, fighting for workers' rights. Eventually the authorities negotiated with Walesa the Gdansk Agreement of August 31, 1980, giving the workers the right to strike and to organize their own independent union.

Walesa didn't stop there. He earned a Nobel Prize in 1983; the government press attacked the award. Parliamentary elections were limited, but they led to the establishment of a non-Communist government. As head of the Solidarity labor union, Walesa began meeting with world leaders. He was the third person in history to address a joint session of the U.S. Congress.[1]

In 1990 he became chairman of Solidarity, then became President of the Republic of Poland.

Walesa knew his fight for freedom would be arduous; he struggled; he suffered, yet he fought. He worked for what he believed in—and didn't allow circumstances to keep him down from what he believed was right. He refused to let someone else steal his personal worth and dignity.

SUMMARIZING PRINCIPLES

1. No one likes to be taken advantage of.

2. Life is full of losers who use, abuse, and confuse others for their own gain.

3. Being taken advantage of chips away at our personal human dignity.

4. Keeping score only invites disadvantaged treatment.

5. Mistreatment of others can be blatant and overt, or it can be subtle and cunning.

6. Some people learn the art of putting others at a disadvantage as a child and carry it into adulthood.

7. It's much easier to see others taking advantage of people than it is to recognize it in our own actions.

MAKING EVALUATION

More than anything else I don't want anyone to take advantage of me. That's really the bottom line regarding ethical behavior.

Here's a word picture of disadvantage: In tennis, one party is always at more of an advantage than another. When a match gets close, the players volley the score back and forth until one player outscores the other. The description used to signal the player closest to the winning point is "advantage." At no other time than the very beginning, at "love," are both players equal.

> *No man can live happily who regards himself alone, who turns everything to his own advantage.*
>
> —SENECA

Unfortunately, we see this sort of advantage/disadvantage all over the world. In fact, you might even see it on a daily basis where you live.

In case you need a refresher, here are some of the ways people are taken advantage of:

- Physically
- Mentally
- Emotionally
- Socially
- Sexually
- Financially

You might even have a few other ways to add to the list, but this is enough to get started.

Sometimes people take advantage of others unwittingly. It becomes a management style people sometimes don't even realize they're using. Consider Jim's story.

Jim works his team hard. He's full of vision and dreams. His company is on an upward climb—he's managed to sustain double-digit growth for more than a decade. He shares bonuses with his employees, and offers generous vacation time.

But his management style is taking a toll. His workers are leaving at an alarming rate. What's he doing wrong?

He's leveraging the company's future value and position on the backs of his most loyal employees. He paints the vision for them to work hard and then they go and work the plan. But for more than five years he has been hinting about selling pieces of the company to the employees. He has never laid out a concrete plan, but he always talks around it—especially when an employee talks about leaving and he wants to win the person back.

Quite simply, he's taking advantage of his employees.

Spotting the Enemy

Users and abusers are people who come up close to take, not to give. Their motive is bad, and the result is usually a sore spot on your soul. Users learn their techniques early, some even as young children.

But spotting them is like spotting a wolf in sheep's clothing—not always easy. Beneath the smile and the fake lamb ears is a vicious soul ready to pounce. Jesus, talking to His followers in the New Testament, told them to be careful of just such people and situations. Obviously, this isn't a new problem.

Jim was very sly about his manipulation. He's what you'd call a *user*. Others are more up-front—they call you when they need something from you, but offer nothing in return. These *abusers* will tell you outright that they need something from you—information, money, help, love, whatever. But they don't wait for you to volunteer it; instead they demand it, using whatever means necessary.

> *Work for something because it is good, not just because it stands a chance to succeed.*
>
> —VACLAV HAVEL

Then there are the *confusers*, those people who just have a way of clouding any situation. And be very clear: it is a tactical maneuver on their part. They know that if they can keep things confusing or keep people at odds with one another, they can steal an advantage.

Pulling the golden ruler from your Power of One toolbox will help you identify this tendency in yourself. Are you a user, abuser, or confuser? Not sure? Ask yourself these questions:

Am I treating others well?
- In other words, am I treating others as I'd like to be treated?
- Am I asking them for things with pure—and transparent—intentions?

Am I treating them right?
- Do I handle all situations with people, whether my spouse, children, friends, or coworkers, ethically?
- Would others say I treat them fairly? Even if they knew my intentions?

Am I communicating truth?
- Do I have to shade the truth or squeeze it a little to get my deal done?
- Am I operating with two sets of books?

If three green lights come up, you're probably treating people the way you would want to be treated. If not, then ask yourself the following:

1. Have you ever been taken advantage of? Describe the situation.

_____

_____

_____

_____

_____

2. What does it feel like to be taken advantage of?

_____

_____

_____

3. Have you ever taken advantage of someone else? What was the situation?

_____

_____

_____

_____

4. Why did I take advantage of people? What was my rationale?

_____

_____

_____

The Power of One means that I come to grips with the fact that I will sometimes be treated unfairly or incorrectly but that will not deter me from the golden walk.

It's not enough to refrain from taking advantage of others. Another way of practicing the Power of One is reacting graciously when others take advantage of you—while not allowing them to walk all over you. Which of the following ways do you usually respond when taken advantage of?

Lash out and get back quick.

Do you practice the eye-for-an-eye style of revenge when others wrong you? Do you speak with a sharp tongue, inflicting pain on others? Do you return bite for bite with quick reflex?

Ignore and deny.

"Oh, they didn't mean to do anything wrong, and honestly, I don't really think they did anything wrong." That's the common refrain of many abuse victims. This quickly turns into a pattern of denial that becomes very destructive to all concerned.

Harbor deep resolve to get revenge.

In this case, a high-octane resentment fuels the fire. Revenge means not just lashing out, but getting back at others. If you take revenge, you'll be taking advantage of others—obviously, not the best tactic.

Become mistrusting of all people.

You see this happen often. People who've been taken advantage of many times over will have a hard time trusting others—even when the people they're with have given them plenty of reason to trust them.

> *Never does the human soul appear so strong and noble as when it forgoes revenge, and dares to forgive an injury.*
>
> —EDWIN HUBBEL CHAPIN

Turn the other cheek.

When someone slaps, this person chooses to keep on moving without letting it faze him. He doesn't stick around, however, for it to happen again—he just forgives and forgets.

Do you see yourself in any of these descriptions? What made you this way? Identify your style—then figure out whether it's really the best style. Obviously, turning the other cheek is ideal. How can you strive to do this?

Areas of Evaluation

It's easier to spot mistreatment when you're prepared for it. Take a moment to identify five ways in which mistreatment and disadvantage could take place in each of these scenarios:

Boss taking advantage of employees

1. _____

2. _____

3. _____

4. _____

Company taking advantage of customers

1. _____

2. _____

3. _____

4. _____

Employees taking advantage of boss

1. _____

2. _____

3. _____

4. _____

Customers taking advantage of company

1. _____

2. _____

3. _____

4. _____

Friend taking advantage of friend

1. _____

2. _____

3. _____

4. _____

TAKING ACTION

The contrast of our feelings associated with being taken advantage of by other people and our rationale for taking advantage of others ourselves is at the heart of the golden rule. We should treat others as we would like to be treated. If we dislike being taken advantage of, then we should refrain from putting others in that situation. Let's do some hard thinking about this subject:

1. In what areas of your life are you in a position to take advantage of another person?

_____

_____

_____

2. Are you a user? An abuser? Or a confuser?

3. What practical steps can you take to implement golden-rule thinking into your decision-making process as you try to avoid taking advantage of others?

_____

_____

_____

4. Do you have any relationships that need mending because you or the other party has been taken advantage of? Which ones?

_____

_____

_____

5. Why do we seek to take advantage of others?

_____

_____

_____

6. How can you put a greater emphasis on valuing others instead of putting your own advancement or material gain first?

_____

_____

_____

7. Sometimes taking advantage is a really gray area. How can you accurately assess what taking advantage of another person is? How can the golden rule help?

_____

_____

_____

_____

8. Make the declaration to not be an abuser, a user, or even a confuser of people.

Learn to say, "I forgive you" when others take advantage of you.
Learn to say, "I will not allow others to use or abuse me."
Learn to say, "I am sorry" when you do treat someone wrongly.

Soldiering, my dear madam, is the coward's art of attacking mercilessly when you are strong, and keeping out of harm's way when you are weak. That is the whole secret of successful fighting. Get your enemy at a disadvantage; and never, on any account, fight him on equal terms. —George Bernard Shaw

Talent Is a Gift; Character Is a Choice

Character is simply long habit continued.

—Plutarch

Driving Thought

The Power of One requires that I steward my own character and integrity and realize that I alone tarnish it.

Drilling Down

Richard Scrushy, founder of HealthSouth Corp., was indicted on eighty-five counts of fraud, money laundering, and other crimes in connection with a $2.7 billion accounting fraud that has nearly bankrupted the company. He was accused of conspiracy, mail fraud, wire fraud, securities fraud, and making false statements.[1]

The man helped build HealthSouth into the biggest U.S. operator of rehabilitation hospitals. The company employed fifty thousand employees at more than seventeen hundred facilities.

What went wrong? People say Scrushy conspired to inflate earnings and launder money to support his lavish lifestyle—a lifestyle that included houses, aircraft, a marina, jewelry, Picasso and Renoir paintings, and a Rolls-Royce and a Lamborghini. He gave generous donations, and his name is emblazoned across a college football stadium, a road, a library, and a Jefferson State Community College campus. He spent big—and prosecutors planned to seize $279 million worth of his assets.

Scrushy made a big name for himself in the business world. He was "successful," but that didn't stop him from failing the biggest test of all—the test of character. He brought down his own name, landed in hot water, and stands to lose plenty of riches.

The worst part: employees lost their jobs, their retirement, and the money they invested. A new management team is now struggling to pay down more than $3 billion in company debt and to avoid bankruptcy. The company stock, which once traded as high as $30 a share, has been closing at lower than $3.

All because of one person's lack of character. All because of greed, corruption of power, and the desire to get more, do more, and be more. Scrushy failed to use his talents for good, and it cost him dearly. That's not what the Power of One is all about. The Power of One condones using power for good—to help others, to build a company, to build yourself—but in a trustworthy, honest, and respectable way. That's a lesson Scrushy—and many other executives in the same boat as him—probably wish they would have learned a long time ago.

Summarizing Principles

1. No one steals another person's character.
2. My character is the only thing that many times distinguishes me from others.
3. Much of character development and character protection goes on in privacy.
4. I must learn to make decisions based on character rather than popularity or public opinion.
5. Good people will ultimately gravitate toward people of good character.

Making Evaluation

Michael S. Josephson and Wes Hanson write in a compilation titled *The Power of Character* (Jossey-Boss, 1998) the following scene. It helps to frame the condition of character in the hearts of some.

I was on a radio talk show and had just quoted some dismal statistics to support my claim that there is a growing hole in our "moral ozone." A man named Bill called in and said that my views were naïve and unrealistic. He said that he had had to cheat in high school to get into college, that he had cheated in college to get a job, and that he occasionally cheats on his job to get ahead. He said my statistics only convinced him he needs to do a better job of teaching his son to cheat. It wasn't the response I had in mind.

And it's probably not the response we would want to hear if we were on a live radio show espousing the golden braids of character. It goes against everything we believe. While this kind of thinking is prevalent—you see it everywhere—not everyone is buying in, thankfully.

Take, for example, the situation going on with an elementary-school system that my friend, a principal, told me about. She shared with me that her staff members had developed a program to instill good character in their students. The school focuses on a different attribute each month, such as respect, punctuality, and courage.

The principal, with thirty years of experience in education, says, "The character trait program our staff has developed is without a doubt the best thing that we have ever done. It has had a major impact on student behavior, student work habits, and achievement."

Focusing on character isn't just for our young people. In fact, it's just as important, if not more so, to develop our character as we mature. In a world full of people trying to get ahead, pushing to better their careers, we all start to look alike. But those who actively work to develop an honest, trustworthy, and kind reputation will stand out from the crowd—and keep themselves from the imbroglios that so many executives find themselves in these days.

Your character affects every aspect of your life. No matter how talented or rich or attractive people are, they will not be able to outrun their characters. And character is one of those things that's truly you—no matter whether you're at home, work, church, or on the ball field coaching your son's Little League team.

> *Men best show their character in trifles, where they are not on guard. It is in insignificant matters, and in the simplest habits, that we often see the boundless egotism which pays no regard to the feelings of others, and denies nothing to itself.*
>
> —ARTHUR SCHOPENHAUER

Here is a list of the ten character traits the elementary school emphasizes. Read each one and then evaluate yourself in light of its description (circle the answer that best describes you):

1. Punctuality—being on time for the requirements of life

        Always   Sometimes   Never

2. Responsibility—being accountable for your behavior

        Always   Sometimes   Never

3. Perseverance—continuing to do something in spite of difficulties or obstacles

        Always   Sometimes   Never

4. Respect—high or special regard; honor one another

        Always   Sometimes   Never

5. Thoughtfulness—consideration of others; courtesy

          Always   **Sometimes**   **Never**

6. Confidence—trust; a feeling of assurance or certainty

          Always   **Sometimes**   **Never**

7. Enthusiasm—strong excitement of feeling

          Always   **Sometimes**   **Never**

8. Courage—standing up for what you believe in; bravery

          Always   **Sometimes**   **Never**

9. Attentiveness—paying heed or care

          Always   **Sometimes**   **Never**

10. Humility—absence of pride or self-assertion; modesty

          Always   **Sometimes**   **Never**

According to the previous evaluation, are you a person who consistently chooses character?

How would others evaluate your character?

_____

_____

Identify a character strength you always choose to display. Why is this so important to you?

_____

_____

_____

Identify a character weakness you struggle with regularly. In what situations do you find yourself struggling with this weakness?

_____

_____

_____

Character Is More Than Talk

Many people talk about doing the right thing, but action is the true measure of character. Dennis Kozlowski, the CEO of Tyco, often touted the frugal way he conducted business and talked about the spartan offices the company maintained. However, anyone who watched his actions closely could have seen that his talk and walk didn't line up. Kozlowski was accused of looting Tyco of $600 million.

We have learned to talk the language of character, but we don't always reinforce it by walking the behavior of character. How closely do your talk and your walk match up?

Talent Is a Gift; Character Is a Choice

There are a lot of things in life a person doesn't get to choose, such as where he's born, who his parents are, and how tall he is. But there are some critical things every person does choose. We choose our faith, our attitude, and our character.

Consider this excerpt from *Leading from the Inside Out: The Art of Self-Leadership* by Samuel D. Rima (Baker Book House, 2000):

> You cannot lead others until you have first led yourself through a struggle with opposing values. When you clarify the principles that will govern your life and the ends that you will seek, you give purpose to your daily decisions. The internal resolution of competing beliefs also leads to personal integrity. And personal integrity is essential to believability. A leader with integrity has one self, at home and at work, with family and with colleagues. He or she has a unifying set of values that guide choices of action regardless of the situation.

Character Brings Lasting Success with People

Trust is essential when working with people. Character engenders trust. People will look past personality and brilliance and hunt down character when they are looking for a real friend or comrade. We all like to be with people who are fun and make us laugh, who are intelligent and make us think, who are inspirational and make us dream, who are confrontational and make us reflect, and who are strong and make us secure.

But all that simply melts to the street and flows down the hill unless these people have true character. What we really look for in a friend or employee are the same traits that our elementary principal is trying to teach the kids in grade school.

Character Doesn't Always Get Rewarded in Our Lifetimes

So why do it? you might ask. Well, it's really quite simple. You develop your character because it's the right thing. When you're living by the good, the right, and the true, you live a life of character—that's just how it works.

Being a person of character doesn't mean expecting applause at a company meeting or a trophy for your good works. You do it, instead, for the sense of peace you feel in doing right and treating others well. It's how you'd want others to treat you, right?

One example of such a determination to do right stems from the sculptors of the Statue of Liberty, a story more than a hundred years old. When the craftsmen and artists who did repairs on the Lady Liberty in 1985–86 studied the statue, they were amazed at the craftsmanship. Frederic Bartholdi and his crew who created her had taken care to finish the statue's crown perfectly, as if everyone would see the top of her head. But a hundred years ago, Bartholdi couldn't have imagined that helicopters would hover over his creation, studying the top of the 151-foot-tall symbol of freedom. He and his crew finished the statue that way because it mattered to them that they did the good, the right, and the true thing. They couldn't have known that anyone else would see their work, but they still did it to perfection. They were working out of their character. Now that's an example to live by![2]

People Can't Rise Above the Limitations of Their Character

There are really only three kinds of people. Those who don't succeed, those who achieve success temporarily, and those who become and remain successful. Having character is the only way to sustain success. Need proof? Just look in the headlines. It seems that every day another executive falls victim to his or her lack of character—and brings down everyone in the company as a result.

But developing character isn't a quick-fix type of thing. It's not something you can grow through a crash-course weekend seminar when one day you realize you need some character. It's impossible. You can't become an astronaut, or a world-class fly fisherman, or an expert brick mason in a microwave weekend of learning. So why should character be any different?

Spend time on it. In the words of H. Jackson Brown, "Talent without discipline is like an octopus on roller skates. There's plenty of movement, but you never know if it's going to be forward, backwards, or sideways."

TAKING ACTION

Confucius asserted, "To know what is right and not do it is the worst cowardice." Character is ultimately a choice. This choice is a holistic endeavor that engages an individual in head, heart, and hand. All three align to produce a person of character.

Character Is a Choice:

Head—choose a guiding principle.

Heart—choose to stand behind it no matter what.

Hand—choose action consistently.

Head

Swiss philosopher Henri Frederic Amiel stated, "He who floats with the current, who does not guide himself according to higher principles, who has no ideal, no convictions—such a man is a mere article of the world's furniture—a thing moved, instead of a living and moving being—an echo, not a voice."

No one wants to be an echo, to live a shadow of a life. Yet that is often the fate of people without convictions. If you desire for your life to have meaning, then you must choose *some* principle to live by.

Character begins in the mind. You need to adopt a guiding standard—one that you can easily understand and implement. A case for the golden rule has been made in this book. Asking, "How would I like others to treat me?" is an effective guideline for any situation. It works in the boardroom, on the ball field, in the classroom, and in the living room. It works with employees, employers, family, and peers. It works whether you are managing a paper route or a Fortune 500 company.

1. Will you adopt the golden rule as your guiding principle? Character starts in the mind.

2. Are you depositing character into your mental warehouse? In other words, are you building and refining your thinking with the good, the right, and the true?

Heart

After you adopt your guiding principle, align your heart behind it—then stay put! Make the guiding principle the foundation upon which you build your decisions. Don't allow circumstance, relational pressure, or promise of pleasure or payoff to sway you. When we align our hearts behind our guiding principles, we resolve to not move. Nineteenth-century novelist George Eliot said, "Keep true, never be ashamed of doing right, decide on what you think is right, and stick to it." The principle is formed in the mind, but it gains its strength in the heart.

1. Will you stand on the golden rule and not allow any person, pressure, or payoff to move you?

2. Do you have passion for good character? How important is a good name and good reputation to you?

Hand

Lastly, character is a choice. We adopt a guiding principle that helps us know what to do. Our hearts give us the courage to resist compromise. It is with our hands that we choose what is right. Ultimately, we don't have character if we don't choose to do what is right.

When we choose to act outside the golden rule, even if we understand the rule and believe in it, then we show a lack of character. As we choose to implement the golden rule through our actions, then we will gain the trust of others and the reputation of character as a result of our consistent choices. Character is especially hard to choose when it hurts—for example, when our choice to live by principle costs us profit, relationship, or popularity. But character is of far greater worth.

1. Are you making good choices every day?
2. How many of your daily choices are based on good character judgments?

Read the following popular quote slowly and out loud. Let each phrase tumble through your brain. Break it into the four rhythms and think about it for a second. Contemplate how true this quote is in your life.

Sow a thought, reap an act. Sow an act, reap a habit. Sow a habit, reap a character. Sow a character, reap a destiny.

Day 18

PRESSURE CAN TARNISH THE GOLDEN TOUCH

It's better to be alone than in bad company.
—GEORGE WASHINGTON

DRIVING THOUGHT

The Power of One holds up under the force of peer pressure.

DRILLING DOWN

Teenagers know peer pressure well. They face it every day in surprisingly high volume, on every subject from hairstyles and lip gloss to sexual activity and drug use. And the majority of teens haven't built up a strong enough sense of self to resist the pressure from their friends.

But as adults, we're expected to be a bit tougher when it comes to peer pressure—and we expect that adults don't pressure their peers quite as much. But that's a pretty tough expectation. For really, pressure to push the ethical limits or to give up under pressure occurs every day in the boardroom, at your desk, or in a sales meeting.

Some might say that Jessica Siegel gave up too early on her fight.[1] Siegel was nearly thirty when she entered the system as an English teacher. Besides teaching, she spent time advising aspiring journalists on the school paper and spent a lot of her time keeping in touch with the kids and their families. She wanted to make a difference.

Samuel Freedman, a former *New York Times* reporter, decided to spend a year observing and writing about life in the local high school where Siegel taught. He interviewed students and sat in the classrooms, and eventually wrote a book on Siegel's experiences.

But what came as a surprise was that when the year finished, Siegel chose not to renew her teaching contract. She quit, and people questioned her motives. Did she need a break? Didn't she care about those kids? Didn't she want to make a difference?

The fact is, she did want to make a difference. And she did in the lives of a few kids. But that might not have been enough for her. She was frustrated with her situation and surroundings and wished she could do more.

Siegel was on the right track. She was working hard, she was connecting with the kids and really starting to get somewhere with some of them. But the pressure of everyday life in the school in which she taught took its toll. There's no faulting Siegel for her decision. It's her life, her choice, and she has her reasons. But this is a good example of how pressure can cause us to collapse, even with the best intentions.

SUMMARIZING PRINCIPLES

1. Pressures can cause either a severe breakdown shatter or a hairline ethics fracture.

2. Our response is usually to crack, melt, or stumble.

3. When we get squeezed, our character flows.

4. Pressure can cause us to lose our Ethical North.

MAKING EVALUATION

According to Linda Treviño, professor of organizational behavior at Penn State's Smeal College of Business Administration, "Ethical breaches are often the result of the corporate culture or pressure from management, pressure that can emerge when a company finds itself unable to live up to financial forecasts or expectations and tries to bend the rules to achieve them."[2]

What kinds of pressures come to us and at us every day? Check out this list. Do you see these in your life?

Deadlines

I know of no business anywhere that doesn't have some kind of deadlines connected with their corporate performance. That being said, deadlines are not the same in weight, speed, or volume. For example, some companies seem to thrive on deadlines, and the entire culture is fueled by one deadline after the next. Newspaper reporters and editors know that all too well.

The demands of every job are going up. Many corporate cultures distinguish between their employees by comparing quality: Who will go the extra mile and stay late again, or come in early again, or do something that helps with the last-minute urgency that a deadline creates?

> *Whenever you find yourself on the side of the majority, it is time to reform (or pause and reflect).*
>
> —MARK TWAIN

Deadlines sometimes become the test for peoples' ethics. The thing that made many a college student cheat on the test was they did not have time to study. Many times deadlines test our ability to be honest and truthful with our bosses, peers, customers, or families.

There are two different deadlines. The first is self-imposed. The more organized a person is, the more of these he or she operates with. Normally these don't test our ethical backbone like a deadline driven by our bosses or our customers, which is the second kind of deadline.

So what do we do?

- Don't cross over the center line of the good, the right, and the true. You will only be driving in head-on-crash territory.

- Don't wait until the last minute to complete a project or follow through on a promise. If someone else waits to the last minute, you can't help that, but you can do something about your own procrastination.

- Don't cave in to any and all demands at the last minute. Learn how to say no or at least navigate the continuous deadline culture correctly.

Peer Pressure

Dennis Rainey, quoting psychologist David Anderregg, made the case that there is no single more influential element in a teenage girl's life than peer pressure. He wrote, "The peak of conformity comes at or around age 13. At this age, there is nothing more important to a child than being just like everyone else—normal."[3]

Over dinner with another couple one evening, my wife and I started talking about the pressure that kids face today. Then the conversation turned to adults, and the obvious was too bold to get around. Adults are just as driven to conform and be normal as a thirteen-year-old girl. We don't outgrow it.

Anyone who has ever had to travel for a job and has peers who travel with him knows he must establish boundaries. The peers will pull and push and continually try to solicit your participation. If the conduct is good, right, and true, then what a bonus. There's no problem. But if the peers are coming from the enemy side of ethics, you have to set up your offensive and defensive game plan just like a college football coach going to his first big Bowl game.

Big Opportunities

Remember, once you get the business, you have to keep the business. To keep the business, you have to service the business, which means you have to give it value. So it is not always a good thing to keep on growing and to always say yes to every opportunity. Only take the ones that you can complete wholeheartedly—and that further your Power of One mind-set.

The allure of the Big Opportunity has always made people turn a little light-headed with their ethics. It sometimes disorients us and keeps us from seeing things as they really are. It might sound good, but is it a Golden Opportunity—or just a big opportunity?

What would you do or say to get the big sale? Would you cheat or shade the good, the right, and the true "just this once"? Many folks do fine with their ethical equilibriums until the big deal shows up. Be careful.

Bad Results or Bad Consequences

This is the same principle that showed up when you were very young and your parents said, "Who did this?" pointing to the chocolate on the carpet. It is amazing how unclear kids can become when they know that honesty will have a penalty. That is when some of us first began to shade the truth.

I cannot change my response just because I know that I am going to get in trouble. I have a friend who is very ethical—until the searchlight is flipped on and he has to sit down and answer the hard questions. He just folds.

In order for me to make good decisions under pressure, I need reminders of what's at stake. First, I'm accountable to God. Second, I'm accountable to my family. And I keep reminders of that around me all the time. In my office I have pictures of my family so I'll never forget that people are depending on me to do right.

> *There is no fire like passion, there is no shark like hatred, there is no snare like folly, there is no torrent like greed.*
>
> —SIDDHARTHA GUATAMA

One of my definitions of success is for those closest to me to love and respect me the most. Reminders are valuable, but they are not enough. I also need systems to keep me on track. For example, if I must make a decision under pressure, I will take the time to write out the problem and solution so I won't act rashly. I also write down promises I make so I cannot easily forget them. I suggest that you do similar kinds of things. Do whatever you must to hold up under pressure.

Pressure can make us do the following:

Crack

There are two kinds of windshield cracks. One is a shattering and the other is a hairline fracture that just works its way across the windshield. Every time you get into your car, it has spread a little farther across the glass. You ask yourself how that can hold up—and how long it can hold up before it falls into your lap.

Pressure in life can do that. It can cause us to either shatter our ethics or just slowly and quietly creep an ethical fracture across the windshield. We crack either in a sudden shatter or we just inch our way across the screens of our lives. The same goes for our ethical framework of life.

Melt

We can also experience a meltdown. It is when our systems become paralyzed. Our shields are down and radars go to a blank screen. We lose all bearings with Ethical North.

The fire of adversity will melt you like butter or temper you like steel. The choice is yours.

—UNKNOWN SOURCE

Stumble

Pressure can also cause us to stumble. We trip up and make a mistake or failure. This is very common. For example, you really never intended to speed. You didn't plan it on purpose, but it still happened. It was a mistake as a result of having left too late to get to that important meeting.

Pressures come in all sizes and shapes and colors. Some are personal and have our names on them. Some are not, but still touch our world.

We all have pressures associated with our work and our life endeavors. We face pressures to produce, to be efficient, to be legal, to be environmentally safe, to be profitable, to meet sales goals, to be free of conflict, and so on. When the pressure to meet these goals causes us to think outside the confines of the golden rule, then we have a problem.

Compromise is often preceded with pressure of some nature. We desire to meet a certain person's expectations and often it means treating another unethically. The goal in living out the golden rule is to handle the pressure appropriately and still maintain our commitment to treating others as we would want to be treated, even among intense pressure.

1. Can you identify with the temptation to compromise under pressure? Name one situation where pressure affected your ethic:

_____

_____

_____

2. What are some pressure points in your work that exert influence on your decisions? Name five:

a.

b.

c.

d.

e.

3. What are the negative outcomes associated with compromising your ethics in order to appease a pressure source?

_____

_____

_____

4. Explain this ancient proverb:

Better a poor man whose walk is blameless than a rich man whose ways are perverse.

_____

_____

_____

5. How do you feel when you compromise under pressure?

_____

_____

_____

6. What could you lose through compromise under pressure?

Work_____

Family_____

Personal_____

Friends_____

TAKING ACTION

Oftentimes the best decisions are made off the battlefield and before the war on our integrity begins. It is helpful to visualize the decisions we will face before we find ourselves in a pressure-packed circumstance. Walk through the following "Am I . . . ?" situations:

- **Am I Going to Make Rash Emotional Decisions?** Pressure creates tension, and tension can make for some emotional moments. Some people have a hard time in such situations, and they make poor decisions that affect themselves or others. How can I guard against that?

- **Am I Going to Compromise the Truth?** Some people find it almost impossible to admit making a mistake. Am I willing to stick with the truth even when it hurts? Remember a half-truth is as bad as a full lie.

- **Am I Going to Take Shortcuts?** Someone once said that the longest distance between two points is a shortcut. While that may be true, pressure tempts us to consider shortcuts when we otherwise wouldn't. Am I willing to fight to do what's good, right, and true?

- **Am I Going to Keep My Commitments?** Moliere said, "Men are alike in their promises. It is only in their deeds that they differ." Am I going to keep my word and follow through, even when it hurts? Will my "promises made, promises kept" slogan melt when the pressure gets really hot?

- **Am I Going to Bow to Others' Opinions?** Some people are especially susceptible to the opinions of others. That was true of me the first five years of my career. Will I do what I know is right, even when it's unpopular? Are you a people pleaser by nature, and do you have to overmanage your opinion poll to keep the good, the right, and the true?

- **Am I Going to Make Promises I Can't Keep?** Samuel Johnson said, "We ought not to raise expectations which it is not in our power to satisfy. It is more pleasing to see smoke brightening into flame, than flame sinking into smoke." How am I going to keep my promises from going up in smoke?

LAST QUESTION

Are you willing to fail to meet others' expectations if it means you keep your integrity? Why or why not?

_____

_____

_____

_____

_____

You never will be the person you can be if pressure, tension and discipline are taken out of your life. —James G. Bilkey

Day 19

PLEASURE CAN TARNISH THE GOLDEN TOUCH

Do not bite at the bait of pleasure till you know there is no hook beneath it.

—THOMAS JEFFERSON

DRIVING THOUGHT

The Power of One means that I don't pursue my own pleasure as my primary goal, and that I don't steal pleasure that doesn't belong to me.

DRILLING DOWN

Deion Sanders, the well-known pro-baseball- and pro-football-star-turned broadcaster, spoke about pleasure in his autobiography, *Power, Money, and Sex: How Success Almost Ruined My Life* (Word, 1998). Deion is a man who has everything and has accomplished things most people don't even dream about. He is the only person in history to play in both a World Series and a Super Bowl. He scored a touchdown in the NFL and hit a home run in major-league baseball in the same week! Not to mention performing a rap song, "It Must Be the Money!" that hit the Top 10 charts.

Deion had all the money and pleasure a man could ever ask for, yet this is what he said in his book: "I tried everything, parties, women, buying expensive jewelry, and gadgets, and nothing helped. I was playing great and every time I turned on the TV I could see myself on three or four commercials, but there was no peace, no joy, just emptiness inside. I tried everything to make me happy and I was emptier than ever. Nothing could satisfy the hunger that was deep down inside of me."

Deion was drilling for pleasure, hoping that it would bring him deep inner satisfaction. It can't. Never could. Never will.

King Solomon from the Old Testament was a man who understood pleasure and pursued it with the kind of dedication that others only dream of. He lived thousands of years ago, and yet his story sounds so much like that of Deion Sanders. The thing that hoisted a person up in King Solomon's culture wasn't sports, but possessions. He had land. He built buildings. He collected art. He bought jewelry. He chased pleasure. He had, for example, a thousand wives, which, as Stewart Briscoe points out, meant many pairs of panty hose hanging in the bathroom.

Over the course of his career, King Solomon denied himself nothing—and could afford to do so—and then he finally concluded that when pursued as an end in itself, pleasure was meaningless and brought as much fulfillment as chasing the wind. The constant chase left him empty.

Solomon does not contend that pleasure is bad or wrong. But he does make the case that it brings little satisfaction on its own. And in the book of Proverbs he gives many examples of stolen pleasure that brings disaster.

> *Anyone who loves pleasure more than truth is headed for trouble—and will take others with him.*

SUMMARIZING PRINCIPLES

1. I must rein in my own appetites and desires to make sure they don't block the path to focusing on others.
2. Pleasure can tarnish even the shiniest example of ethics.
3. Pleasure operates like a lure to a fish to snag us, then tugs us away from our ethical compass.
4. Battling the beast of pleasure is a never-ending fight.
5. Pleasure chasing never delivers the fulfillment it promises.

MAKING EVALUATION

The Tarnishing Process

What does it mean to tarnish? It means to become discolored, dull, spoiled, or tainted. We know what it means, but when does it happen? It is a process, not an event. You can't point to the silver bowl and see it the moment it tarnishes. But one day you'll put the bowl in the cabinet, looking fine as always. Then the next time you pull it out, you'll notice it has tarnished.

When our Ethical Core tarnishes, here's what happens:

The bad begins to appear good.
The wrong begins to feel right.
The false begins to seem true.

When those things happen, you can rest assured you're tarnishing. Your ethical center is no longer golden, but is now discolored, dull, and spoiled. Doesn't sound too attractive, does it?

We must remember that pleasure is always momentary. You won't find true contentment in life's pleasures. Yet at the same time, the lure of money, sex, power, drunkenness, and other pleasure sources is very strong. So strong, in fact, that many people are willing to trade things of long-term value for the short-term sensation of pleasure. Some trade the long-term contentment found in faithfulness for the momentary pleasure of an affair. Others trade the long-term contentment found in hard work and honesty for quick riches found in insider trading. The problem is that after the momentary buzz of a pleasurable situation fades, there is usually a hefty price of consequence to pay in the end.

> *There is no odor so bad as that which arises from goodness tainted.*
> —HENRY DAVID THOREAU

Sports Illustrated reported that Mike Price, the former coach of the University of Alabama football program, found the power of pleasure devastating. Only on the job for a few months, Price was publicly exposed after a night of drinking and attending strip clubs while on a trip to Florida in which he was representing the University. Coach Price lost his coveted coaching position and was released from his unsigned multimillion-dollar contract. Not to mention the effects on his family and reputation. His trials remind us that pleasure may pay off in the immediate future, but can cause us to compromise what matters most.

1. List five to seven pleasures that people often seek.

_____

_____

_____

_____

2. How could seeking pleasure tarnish our ability to live out the golden rule?

_____

_____

_____

3. Why do you think pleasure is so alluring?

_____

_____

_____

4. Evaluate yourself. Are there any particular pleasures that could tempt you to compromise the golden rule? What are they?

_____

_____

_____

5. In seeking after these pleasures, what need are you trying to fulfill? Is there a proper way to fulfill this need that avoids compromise?

_____

_____

TAKING ACTION

In light of the power of pleasure and our strong desires toward it, consider the following suggested plan for combating the temptations we face:

Step 1: Avoid Temptation

Mark Twain observed, "There are several good precautions against temptation, but the surest is cowardice." If you know you are especially susceptible to a pleasure that would tempt you to cross an ethical line, put yourself out of harm's way. When you see it coming, cross to the other side of the street. The best way to avoid temptation is to prevent it.

For example, many businessmen and women who struggle with infidelity or sexual immorality make it a point to not travel on business without their spouses. Or, many will find a trusted colleague to serve as an accountability partner while away on trips. Although not every work situation has an easy solution to counter regular temptations, there is always a better path.

Name a few places, things, or even people that you need to avoid in order to resist temptation to compromise your ethics.

1. _____

2. _____

3. _____

4. _____

If your job or circumstance requires you to be in a situation you find tempting, how can you work toward changing the situation or at least minimizing the potential for failure?

_____

_____

_____

_____

_____

Do you know anyone who has ever made significant career adjustments just to keep his or her integrity and ethics? Who was it and what was his or her story? How can you apply that story to your life?

_____

_____

_____

_____

_____

Step 2: Practice Discipline

The second key is to develop discipline. In living out the golden rule, we must execute right choices in the face of temptation. In a culture that tells us "if it feels good, do it," we must be disciplined enough to stick to our guiding principles.

In *Reasons to Be Glad,* author Richard Foster writes:

The disciplined person is the person who can do what needs to be done when it needs to be done. The disciplined person is the person who can live in the appropriateness of the hour. The extreme ascetic and the glutton have exactly the same problem: they cannot live appropriately; they cannot do what needs to be done when it needs to be done. The disciplined person is the free person. It's ironic, but to gain freedom, you need to contain your emotions with discipline.

1. What is the payoff for doing the right thing? Think about specific times and situations in which you could have taken the easy route—the wrong one—but you stuck it out and did the right thing. What was your payoff? Was there an obvious payoff or consequence you avoided?

2. How can others help you in being disciplined? Do you need an accountability partner to ask you the tough questions? Can you ask friends, your spouse, or colleagues to not invite you to functions that are too tempting to your vices, for example?

3. Discipline sticks to the plan even when you are assured that you won't get caught or will go unnoticed. Can you name any situations you are in that are "under the radar" of others' scrutiny?

4. How can you assure discipline in these areas?

_____

_____

_____

_____

Step 3: Delay Gratification

We are microwave people; we want everything now. We feel we have a God-given right to never be bored, always be happy, and always have it our way. It's our right as Americans, right? The truth is that this line of thinking is very dangerous. A person who feels as though immediate gratification is a necessity is destined for compromise.

Our grandparents taught us that, "good things come to those who wait." There is a lot of truth to be found in that simple phrase. We must convince ourselves that we do not have to partake in every pleasure offered to us.

Pleasure is maximized when it is experienced in the proper context. Outside of the proper context, pleasure leads to pain.

> *I took a course in speed waiting. Now I can wait an hour in only ten minutes.*
> —STEVEN WRIGHT

1. How does the concept of delayed gratification feel to you?

_____

_____

2. What are the benefits of delaying pleasure until you can enjoy it in its proper context?

_____

_____

GOLDEN CHALLENGE

Pick an area of pleasure in your life (such as eating a certain item) and deny yourself that pleasure for a time. After you go without, process the difference from your normal experience.

Step 4: See the End Result

If we allow it to, the desire for pleasure (or comfort) will talk us into doing things we will regret afterward. Pleasure often promises what it cannot deliver. Many people have been consumed by engaging in certain behaviors or activities only to find those very activities are destroying their lives. Very few junkies thought about the devastating effects of getting high the first time. Few pornography addicts thought of the depth of their sickness when they sneaked their first glimpse of a perverse magazine. The lure of pleasure is the promise of goodness with no regrets. The truth is that there are always consequences for our actions. It is a lie to believe we ever get away with anything. Our last step in avoiding the pleasure trap is to focus on the consequence and not the payoff.

> *Everybody, sooner or later, sits down to a banquet of consequences.*
>
> —ROBERT LOUIS STEVENSON

Fill in the following chart:

Source of pleasure	Payoff	Possible consequence
"Cooking the books"	Increased profit	Company ruin

Evaluate the situation. Is risking your integrity worth the momentary payoff in light of the long-term consequence?

Aesop, that master storyteller of old, told this fable:

A jar of honey was upset in a housekeeper's room, and a number of flies were attracted by its sweetness. Placing their feet in it, the flies ate greedily. Their feet, however, became so smeared with honey that they could not use their wings, nor release themselves, and they were suffocated. Just as they were dying, they exclaimed: "Oh, foolish creatures that we are, for the sake of a little pleasure we have destroyed ourselves."

Pleasure, when it is a man's chief purpose, disappoints itself; and the constant application to it palls the faculty of enjoying it.
—Richard Steele

Day 20

POWER CAN TARNISH THE GOLDEN TOUCH

Nearly all men can stand adversity, but if you want to test a man's character, give him power.

—ABRAHAM LINCOLN

DRIVING THOUGHT

The Power of One means that I keep a close watch on how I think about power and how I use it.

DRILLING DOWN

As Special Counsel to the president, Charles Colson lived in a world of power, and the misuse of that available authority landed him in prison.

Colson landed his dream job—that as one of four special aides to President Nixon—in 1969. He was named the liaison between outside interest groups and inside policy makers. In media circles, Colson was known as the White House "hatchet man," a man feared by even the most powerful politicos during his four years of service to President Nixon.

Then *The New York Times* published portions of the Pentagon Papers, a top-secret report on America's involvement with Vietnam, and revealed that U-2 surveillance planes had flown secret assignments over China. Nixon directed Colson to form a group to prevent such sensitive leaks in the future. Colson tapped Howard Hunt and G. Gordon Liddy for the job.

Then people suspected that laws had been broken, and then the discovery of the secret taping system that Nixon had activated allowed the truth and proof to surface. Nixon resigned the presidency—the only man to ever do so—and a number of administration personnel went to jail.

Colson was one of those who ended up behind bars because of his involvement with the Pentagon Papers, and has been most vocal about how easy it became to use power for personal advantage. He considers his time in jail time well spent. It was that experience that revolutionized his life, and prepared him for a second career of working with men and women in prison.

The recently released portions of the Nixon tapes reveal a president who was crass, profane, and quick to call for investigations on those who opposed the administration—or whom Nixon simply did not like. Even Nixon supporters who have listened to the tapes have been shocked.

It is very difficult for people with power available to them to steward it correctly. Proper use of power takes character and righteous determination. For, as U.S. President John Adams said, "No man is wise enough or good enough to be trusted with unlimited power."

Power is like a strong-flowing river. As long as it keeps its course, it is a useful thing of beauty. But when it floods its banks, it brings great destruction. How does one keep it in its banks? Take the advice of U.S. President Harry Truman. He recommended, "If a man can accept a situation in a place of power with the thought that it's only temporary, he comes out all right. But when he thinks he is the cause of the power, that can be his ruination." Anyone who realizes that he's guarding his power too much had better start examining himself for breaches of ethics. Power can be terribly seductive.

SUMMARIZING PRINCIPLES

1. Whether we realize it or not, we all have a certain amount of power.

2. Power is never an end in itself. Like money, it is a tool used to influence someone, to help a cause, to right a wrong, to create an opportunity.

3. Power is a sacred trust.

4. The more power we give away, the more powerful we become.

5. Personal power and positional power must never be confused. Both can be abused or neglected.

MAKING EVALUATION

Power comes in many forms: dollars, position, numbers, knowledge, competence. Regardless of the package, bow, and delivery system, it must be respected and treated as a fragile explosive agent.

Whether it places us over a hundred thousand employees, a whole nation, or two young kids at home, we all have some measure of power. Power is a sacred trust. It doesn't matter if we inherit our power, if we attain it gradually as we rise through the corporate ranks, or if we receive it by virtue of being elected to a post. Whatever the case, it doesn't really belong to us, and we have no guarantee it will last. The only thing we know for sure is that, for as long as we have it, we are responsible for using it wisely.

There is positional power and personal power. Positional power comes and goes. Positional power comes from the titles we hold, the offices we work from, the cars we drive, the salaries we bring home, the neighborhoods where we live, and the like. It is externally driven and comes for a while then goes and makes its home at someone else's address. The sooner we can learn the reality that positional power does not belong to us personally, the better power brokers we will become.

Personal power, however, is based on moral authority. It represents a source of energy that flows from the inside out. Unlike positional power, it *does* belong to us. Personal power is founded upon who we are, not what we do, where we live, what we own, or who we know.

Personal power and positional power must never be confused. Both can be abused or neglected. Both can be used to advance the good, the right, and the true.

Read the following statements and then react to them as you look at your own life:

> *Anyone entrusted with power will abuse it if not also animated with the love of truth and virtue, no matter whether he be a prince, or one of the people.*
>
> —JEAN DE LA FONTAINE

Statement: Many abuses of power are a result of one receiving power too early.

1. When is a person ready for power?

2. Are you ready to receive power?

3. In what areas do you need to mature to be a more responsible holder of power?

_____

_____

_____

Statement: The preservation of power is often a source of ethical compromise.

1. How could keeping yourself in power lead to bending the golden rule?

_____

_____

_____

2. Have you ever been tempted to pursue self-preservation of power instead of using it to better the organization? When?

_____

_____

_____

Statement: _Power is bestowed upon a person for service, yet many in power develop a sense of entitlement or privilege and begin to believe that he or she and the institution are one._

1. How can power be used to serve oneself instead of the organization?

_____

_____

_____

2. Have you ever been tempted to use your power to benefit yourself at the cost of the organization? How did you come to think this was OK?

_____

_____

_____

Statement: _Power is to be viewed as a temporary gift, but when one begins to think he is the cause of the power and not the recipient, then compromise is forthcoming._

1. How can we hold on to the power we have received with a sense of personal responsibility and not believe that the organization revolves around us?

_____

_____

_____

2. Which is more important to you: the preservation of the organization or the promotion of self?

Power is never an end in itself. Like money, it is a tool—to influence someone, to help a cause, to right a wrong, or to create an opportunity. The more power we give away, the more powerful we become.

TAKING ACTION

We all have some level of influence or power. We can use that power for good and benefit our organizations and those around us. We can also abuse that power and use it for ourselves at the cost of our organization and others. The golden rule will guard against this very thing. Work through the following exercises to think more deeply about how to live out the golden rule with your power.

> *A great man is one who can have power and not abuse it.*
> —HENRY L. DOHERTY

1. Do an analysis of your positional power and your personal power.

   • My positional power looks like:

   _____

   _____

   _____

   _____

   _____

   _____

   • My personal power looks like:

   _____

   _____

   _____

   _____

   _____

   _____

2. Name five ways to use your power to benefit others and your organization:

a. _____

b. _____

c. _____

d. _____

e. _____

3. Name five ways your power could be abused:

a. _____

b. _____

c. _____

d. _____

e. _____

4. Can you name a role model who exemplifies using his or her power in light of the golden rule? Why did you pick this person?

_____

_____

_____

5. Name three ways to counteract the thought that power brings with it privilege.

_____

_____

_____

6. Can you think of a situation in which power is abused for personal gain on a regular basis in your organization? Write about it here.

_____

_____

_____

7. How can you break this ongoing cycle?

_____

_____

_____

_____

No man is wise enough or good enough to be trusted with unlimited power. —John Adams

Day 21

Pride Can Tarnish the Golden Touch

In general, pride is at the bottom of all great mistakes.
—John Ruskin

Driving Thought

The Power of One means that I never let my pride elevate me above others and make everything all about me.

Drilling Down

Patrick Lencioni had no idea his book would get the traction that it has. Naturally, his publisher hoped it would. But with the volume of printed material hitting the streets every week, who would have ever guessed that *The Five Temptations of the CEO* would have made such a national sound? In his book Lencioni identifies five things that all CEOs struggle with:

Temptation 1—Choosing Status over Results

Temptation 2—Choosing Popularity over Accountability

Temptation 3—Choosing Certainty over Clarity

Temptation 4—Choosing Harmony over Productive Conflict

Temptation 5—Choosing Vulnerability over Trust

Each of these temptations carries real dangers for a leader. Think about the world of a CEO as you digest more of his thinking.

Temptation 1—Choosing Status over Results

Worrying about how much public recognition one receives is a possible sign of susceptibility to the first temptation. Although human nature dictates that we hope for a just share of acknowledgment, it is a dangerous part of human nature to entertain. Certainly, at one time or another all CEOs have experienced short shrift when it comes to public recognition. Those who eventually get their recognition are the CEOs who aren't distracted by the occasional slighting that an unscientific press is sure to give. Interestingly enough, they experience a low degree of satisfaction from such press. After all, they take larger personal satisfaction from achieving results.

Temptation 2—Choosing Popularity over Accountability

It is wonderful for CEOs to care about direct reports as people, so long as they can separate the success of those relationships from their sense of self-esteem and personal happiness. This is difficult because most of us try to avoid major disagreements with friends, and it is impossible not to be concerned about a deep rift with one of them. If those close friends are your direct reports, the accountability within the organization can be threatened. The slightest reluctance to hold someone accountable for his or her behaviors and results can cause an avalanche of negative reaction from others who perceive even the slightest hint of unfairness or favoritism.

Temptation 3—Choosing Certainty over Clarity

It is no surprise that many CEOs take a great deal of pride in their analytical and intellectual acumens. Unable to realize that their success as executives usually has less to do with intellectual skills than it does with personal and behavioral discipline, they spend too much time debating the finer points of decision making.

Temptation 4—Choosing Harmony over Productive Conflict

Productive executive staff meetings should be exhaustive inasmuch as they are passionate, critical discussions. Every meeting has conflict. Some executives just sweep that conflict under the table and let employees deeper in the organization sort it out. This doesn't happen by accident.

Temptation 5—Choosing Vulnerability over Trust

No one loves to be wrong, but some people hate it. Great CEOs don't lose face in the slightest when they are wrong because they know who they are, they know why they are CEOs, and they realize the organization's results, not the appearance of being smart, are their ultimate measure of success. They know that the best way to get results is to put their weaknesses on the table and invite people to help them minimize those weaknesses. Overcoming this temptation requires a degree of fear and pain that many CEOs are unwilling to tolerate.

Why did the book *The Five Temptations of the CEO* hit such a home run in our culture? Well, folks a lot smarter and with more at stake have spent time to figure that one out. I'm not certain, but my guess is one of the following:

1. It is a very well-written book.

2. It is immediately practical.

3. It triggers our fascination with the top of the corporate pyramid.

4. It is something that can be applied to every one of us no matter what title we carry.

The last one is the real fuel. When something touches all of us, it finds front-page space. For example, 9/11, the presidential debate, a war, anthrax, and the stock-market roller coaster have hit home for many of us in one way or another.

After rereading *The Five Temptations of the CEO*, I wanted to sit down and write a book called *The One Temptation of EHBA (Every Human Being Alive)*. It would not replace Lencioni but act as the primer to be thought about as a background. There is a sickness that every human being faces on a daily basis. It is a spiritual flu of sorts. It is called pride. Ken Blanchard calls it the greatest addiction in the world today—the human ego.

Pride is the one muscle that is at full strength in kids and parents, in bosses and employees, in buyers and sellers, in rich and in poor, in all of us. It masks itself in a million different outfits, but it is easy to spot and always carries the same card; it is about *me*.

SUMMARIZING PRINCIPLES

1. Pride wants to constantly be in the center of the stage with all spotlights on it.

2. Becoming more secure in my own self can settle the ego appetite deep within us that fuels our pride.

3. Placing attention on others starves the "me, me, me" appetite in all of us.

4. Pride that is watered and fed will grow to be a powerful destructive animal that will lead us to a fall.

MAKING EVALUATION

A few years ago I attended a neighbors meeting to start a baseball league for dads and their boys. A former college-baseball stud had the vision and the plan to launch a small league that would help dads spend time with their boys and allow neighbors to get to know each other. I was invited to the information meeting to talk through the idea. About a dozen dads showed up. The meeting was going fine until a certain spirit took over.

Dads began to get their competitive juices going, and there was a little physical and verbal strutting taking place in Bill's living room. And then finally someone played the in-house umpire and called a foul. Bill regained control of the floor and said, "Fellows, fellows . . . This is not about you! It is about your boy. Can we restart the meeting and get them in the middle of the circle instead?"

It's not about me. Boy, that's a hard pill to swallow.

The question always arises. Is all pride bad? No. There can be a good side to this dangerous muscle. But even the good expression can suddenly get sucked down the pipe of the dark spirit of pride.

When a young girl stands up for her convictions and says no to immorality because she has pride in herself, we would all stand and applaud her. At least every dad I know would. When an employee decides to go the extra mile and redo the presentation because it just doesn't meet the standard of the company and his pride in the excellent standard his company has drives him, we all say terrific. Give that person a bonus.

> *There is perhaps not one of our natural passions so hard to subdue as pride.*
>
> —BENJAMIN FRANKLIN

But that is not what we are talking about when we talk about the temptation of pride. We are talking about the spirit and the energy we all have to make life rotate around our world and us.

Pride goes bad when it gobbles up all the attention and doesn't share the praise and recognition around the office.

Pride goes bad when it really thinks you did it all by yourself with no help from anyone.

Pride goes bad when it practices the "invented here" mentality.

Pride goes bad when it looks down in arrogance on others for any reason.

Pride goes bad when it takes credit where credit isn't due.

Pride goes bad when it takes the focus off the person in need.

Pride goes bad when it looks out for number one all the time.

Pride goes bad when it showers praise on others (often ostentatiously) and primarily in hopes that its kindness will be noticed and is itself praised.

Nineteenth-century writer and art critic John Ruskin asserted, "Pride is at the bottom of all great mistakes."

What is it about pride that is so negative? Professor, writer, and Christian apologist C. S. Lewis offered a perspective on pride with great insight. He believed that pride leads to every other vice. He remarked:

Does this seem to you exaggerated? If so, think it over. I pointed out a moment ago that the more pride one had, the more one disliked pride in others. In fact, if you want to find out how proud you are the easiest way is to ask yourself, "How much do I dislike it when other people snub me, or refuse to take any notice of me?" . . . The point is that each person's pride is in competition with everyone else's pride. It is because I wanted to be the big noise at the party that I am so annoyed at someone else being the big noise. . . . Now what you want to get clear is that pride is essentially competitive, is competitive by its very nature, while the other vices are competitive only, so to speak, by accident.

We say that people are proud of being richer, or more clever, or better looking than others. If everyone else became equally rich or clever or good-looking, then there would be nothing to be proud about. It is the comparison that makes you proud: the pleasure of being above the rest.

At the heart of pride is competition and comparison. In our pride we strive to be better than our neighbor. How can people treat others as they want to be treated if their preoccupation is to beat them? They can't. In fact, if your goal is to be richer, smarter, or better looking than everyone else, your focus is entirely on yourself and your self-interests. Pride can blind you—to your own faults, to other people's needs, and to ethical pitfalls that lie in your path.

> *Pride gets no pleasure out of having something, only out of having more of it than the next man.*
>
> —C. S. LEWIS

1. Who or what is the central focus of your life?

2. What is the difference in pride and confidence?

3. Which of the following pictures most accurately represents you?

4. What is the main conflict between pride and the golden rule?

_____

_____

_____

5. How can removing the focus from self benefit you?

_____

_____

_____

6. How much time do you spend comparing yourself to others?

_____

TAKING ACTION

Counteracting pride is not an easy thing. Self-preservation and promotion are imprinted on our human DNA. Our focus is to contain and direct these within appropriate boundaries. Consider a dose of the "Be's" in light of our study on pride:

Be Warned!

Pride comes before a fall. Surely you have heard this phrase before and many of us have seen it in action. It ought to act as a flashing yellow light of caution.

It is said that victorious Roman generals had slaves riding with them on their victory parade, whispering, "You are only mortal; you are only mortal" as the crowds cheered. Why? Because we all have a tendency to puff up with pride.

> *Pride is the only disease known to man that makes everyone sick except the person who has it.*
>
> —BUDDY ROBINSON

1. Describe how pride can be a seed that grows to bear the fruit of calamity.

_____

_____

2. How could pride sink you?

_____

_____

_____

_____

3. Has pride ever sunk you?

_____

Be Humble!

Give up your rights. In order to remove the focus from yourself, lose your right to always win or be on top. Remember, it's not about you. In a sea of more than six billion people, life does not revolve around you, your desires, and your needs.

1. Is humility a personality type, an attitude, or an action?

_____

2. What is false humility?

_____

_____

3. How should a humble person view himself, his organization, and his world?

_____

_____

_____

_____

Be Outward Focused!

A prideful person cannot take in the success of others. Yet the golden rule pushes us to not only revel in others' successes, but to enable them.

1. How can you encourage those around you when they succeed?

_____

_____

_____

2. How can you help others around you to win?

_____

_____

_____

_____

Disciplining yourself to do what you know is right and important, although difficult, is the highroad to pride, self-esteem, and personal satisfaction. —Brian Tracy

Day 22

PRIORITIES CAN TARNISH THE GOLDEN TOUCH

Things that matter most must never be at the mercy of things that matter least.

—JOHANN WOLFGANG VON GOETHE

DRIVING THOUGHT

The Power of One occurs when I keep the main things . . . the main things.

DRILLING DOWN

No matter what our mission statement says, a for-profit company has "make a profit" high on its list of priorities. Otherwise, what would the motivation behind that company be? To lose money?

We all understand that making money is a part of business. That's an acceptable business standard. But is it above everything else? It shouldn't be. Just ask the company outlined below how well making money priority number one worked for them:

As a social membership with high-dollar rates, the company mandated ironclad membership contracts. However, state law provided a three-day think-it-over period in which customers could cancel anything without a penalty.

This club, however, wanted to inflate their sales figures to meet sales numbers, look good for an upcoming buyout by a multinational corporation, and earn the sales manager a company car bonus. So they regularly took the full thirty days they had by law—the practice was entirely legal—to refund a customer's money. The amount of a refund ran between $500 and $3,700. The company had about a 10 percent cancellation rate. And for a medium-sized company, that adds up to a nice chunk of change. Until refunded, that amount showed up in the company's monthly sales report.

Customers may not have liked waiting for their refunds, but the company was doing nothing wrong legally. But problems arose when an angry customer contacted a local television station to complain, resulting in an exposé. A local newspaper, the national newswire, and eventually the NBC-TV program *Dateline* picked up the story about membership scams—never once mentioning that what the company was doing was entirely legal, though certainly frustrating to customers.[1]

As a result of the media exposure, monthly sales slowed by 40 percent, and cancellations doubled. And, though the company was purchased, as expected, the new management team could not salvage the business and was forced to sell it back to franchisees for a greatly reduced rate.

The lesson here is that, while what they were doing was clearly legal, it was obviously not in the company's best interests. Sure, the sales managers wanted to boost numbers—a short-term hurrah—but they lost sight of the fact that without customers, they'd have no sales at all. None. They put money—not people—as their top priority. And they paid dearly for that mistake. Companies and individuals must learn to keep the main things . . . the main things.

> *You can't build a reputation on what you're going to do.*
> —HENRY FORD

Sorting and ranking the priorities of life is not always easy whether you are one person or a whole company. Knowing that one opportunity or assignment really ranks ahead of another is sometimes challenging. Among the things that a good leader has to provide his company today is the guidance on priorities. Sorting and sifting, then measuring and ranking, are very critical and very beneficial. Everything can't be number one on the list, and everything can't carry the same strategic return.

SUMMARIZING PRINCIPLES

1. How we live, rather than how we talk or how we dream, reflects our priorities.
2. Priority living sometimes begins by unlearning certain popular and conventional thinking on life.
3. All pursuits in life are not equal.
4. Lean into the sobering moments when life shuts down to realign and make course corrections.
5. An unreasonable, unworkable, unethical schedule of life's priorities is never sustainable.
6. Bringing order and peace to my private world always helps center my public world.

MAKING EVALUATION

How we live, rather than how we talk or how we dream, reflects our priorities.

You can talk all you want, but when it comes down to it, it's what you do that matters. Say you have two people working for you. They both bring great ideas to the table, but one of them forgets to follow up on those great ideas the moment the conference room door bursts open. The other returns to her desk and immediately figures out how to incorporate the ideas and decisions into her daily life. Which employee would you respect more—and turn to the next time you wanted something done? Exactly.

A dreamer is just that. Allow yourself to dream, but make it a priority to act on those dreams. Show people, including yourself, that you're just as much a doer as a dreamer.

Priority living sometimes begins by unlearning certain popular and conventional thinking on life.

Often in life we have to unlearn and unpack previous misconceptions before we can move forward in the right direction. Where did you collect your data that helps you sort life's priorities? Starting off with the right point of view helps us practice the Power of One.

Jimmy Carter learned a great deal from his mother, Lillian Carter, about how to relate to people different from himself. Those values—priorities in his mother's life—modeled the priorities he showed while president of the United States.

The Carter family lived in a small community in Georgia during a time when blacks were oppressed. His mother was a nurse who gave much of the money she made in that profession to blacks in the community who needed medicine. She also opened her home to the

> *Words show a man's wit but actions his meaning.*
>
> —BENJAMIN FRANKLIN

blacks—something Jimmy's father, Earl, disapproved of. But that didn't stop Lillian, and it didn't stop Jimmy from learning his mother's values.

Taking care of the oppressed was central to Lillian's life, and those priorities were passed on directly to Jimmy. It was a strictly segregated community. It was an accepted situation, but Lillian didn't pay any attention to it. Black neighbors came to her because she was, in effect, the only doctor they had, said Carter.[2]

Luckily for our country, Jimmy Carter took after his mother's priorities—not his father's.

Because of this he didn't have to unpack bad thinking on the area of inclusion and diversity. He actually started believing the good, the right, and the true early in life, which made the practice of the good, the right, and the true easier. We all have collected the raw material that has helped us frame up our thinking on what is top priority in life—and what we can allow to sift to the bottom.

All pursuits in life are not equal.

I had an email message the other day. It said simply, "What real benefit is it if a man gains the whole world but loses his soul?" The friend who sent it said that he'd been thinking about that quote and just wanted to share it.

> *Decide what you want, decide what you are willing to exchange for it. Establish your priorities and go to work.*
>
> —H. L. HUNT

It made me start thinking that, even when we're busy in our lives doing good, some good is better than other good. All pursuits in life are not equal. For example, some will require more of me—and some will return more to me. Some pursuits will allow me to practice the Power of One more easily—and some are more self-centered. My friend's message helped me to remember what's important in life, and start to tune out priorities that aren't so important.

Lean into the sobering moments when life shuts down to realign and make course corrections.

Jim's assistant called me on my cell phone and said that our Monday session was going to be cut short because Jim was scrambling with last-minute clients and customers. On top of that Jim had to go out of town on an unplanned emergency to be with his father, who had been admitted into the hospital.

Jim is a CEO that I have been coaching for a few months. He is hard-charging and posting record growth and profits. His company is shaking and baking his whole industry. And Jim is in transition with his life. Not a career transition, mind you, but a priority transition.

So we met for lunch. It was an amazing hour and a half. Jim gave me an update on his world and we tackled a couple of issues, like normal. But I sensed Jim had something in his pocket, as it were.

He waved off some of the normal things we might talk through and said he wanted to show me something. Jim pulled out a masterpiece. A one-page document that had captured his thinking and reflection from the last week, where he had spent much of his time sitting in the halls, rooms, and cafeteria of the hospital where his father lay.

Jim opened the discussion by saying, "You ever see any of those trend charts in magazines or newspapers that graph on one page what is in and what is out? I had a lot of time that I could not be on the phone or the computer, so I spent time with myself and those around me who really matter to me." He said he and his wife processed this together and he wanted to show me.

I had a sense that this wasn't just some scribbled note thrown together on the way to a meeting. This water was flowing from a deep well that tapped into some rare and pure water at the core of Jim. Here is his priority list for life:

OUT	IN
Vision	Dream
Purpose	Passion
Significant	Insignificant
Authoring	Talking/listening
David/Moses/Nehemiah	John the Baptist/Barnabas
Build people	Inspire people
Save time	Spend time
Knowledge	Wisdom
Out there	Here
Intentions	Behavior

These words are nothing brilliant. And they might not mean anything to you or me. But they represent a seismic shift in Jim's perspective and priorities. He showed movement and development. He was able to get a handle on who he is and had been, and then he was able to identify a new world reality for him.

Measuring things against eternity and measuring things during the sober moments of life is very important. Putting things in your life in perspective helps realign your priorities. Even the best of cars gets out of alignment after driving. Life is the same way; a few bumps, potholes, and ditches can throw your life out of alignment. It's up to you to take time to realign it, as Jim did.

An unreasonable, unworkable, unethical schedule of life's priorities is never sustainable.

Constructing a reasonable and workable approach to life balance is the first step toward successful priority living. Many people rush to make a quick adjustment in their priorities, but rash decisions leave them disappointed or rejected. It often starts with the noble interest of realigning life correctly. But their attempt is to create a short list of how life should line up. It is top-down, linear, and idealistic. Does this sound familiar?

1. Faith
2. Family
3. Work
4. Recreation and hobbies

Sounds perfect. But how realistic is it, really? Life just doesn't arrange itself in neat little boxes that are predictable and controllable. You might say you put your family toward the top—but what happens when a looming deadline consumes all of your "spare" time?

And who ever feels as if they've done enough with the husband and daddy roles that they can say, "OK, I've completed that for the day. Now I'm going to go do the work thing." Really, even if you could do that, how do the thirty minutes in the morning and two hours in the evening really compare with the eight to ten hours you spend at work each day? They just don't.

It's just not possible to always "do life" in the order you think it should go. Life isn't a "check it off the list and move on" proposition. Instead, it's figuring out how to live all of those things at once.

> *Time ripens all things.*
> *No man's born wise.*
>
> —MIGUEL DE CERVANTES

Life is more about setting our hearts on things that really matter—and then making sure that we live our lives, juggling all of those things on a daily basis with a lot of give and take with the flow and rhythms of life. A more reasonable and workable model is to identify the balls in life that you have to juggle on a regular basis—then figure out how to keep them all in the air at once.

Just remember that adopting a method that is unreasonable and unworkable is very discouraging. When setting goals, make them realistic and reasonable and you'll have a better chance of succeeding. But don't make the mistake of setting goals too low, either. Adopting a method that is unethical will end with disappointment.

Bringing order and peace to my private world always helps center my public world.

Gordon MacDonald first described the difference for me. He said that a "called" person and a "driven" person are not the same. Distinguishing the difference and then converting from a driven man (or woman) to a called man (or woman) can help navigate the perilous waters of priority living. A driven person is:

- most often gratified only by accomplishment
- preoccupied with the symbols of accomplishment
- usually caught in the uncontrolled pursuit of expansion
- someone with an often-limited regard for integrity
- often limited or undeveloped
- highly competitive
- often full of volcanic anger
- abnormally busy

Based on this list, would you say that your core is fueled by drive? Or does energy more consistent with "calling" fuel you?

You can't walk into a bank and attain a small-business loan without a business plan. If you told the loan officer that you were just looking to spend some time working so that the days would pass by quicker, you would surely be rejected. None of us would launch a business without a plan that included our goals and strategies. Yet many of us live our personal lives with little intentional planning. We are carried by opportunity or cultural winds with little examination as to why we are drifting this way or that way.

> *A man must drive his energy, not be driven by it.*
>
> —WILLIAM FREDERICK BOOK

What gets you out of bed in the morning? What makes you pound the table with passion? What are you seeking to accomplish in life?

Envision your funeral. This is a morbid thought, but visualize what you would want to hear said about your life and your legacy. If you died tomorrow, what would people say about you? Would it make you proud of the way you lived? Consider this old saying: *If you want to know how to live your life, think about what you'd like people to say about you after you die—then live backward.*

Thinking about how we will be remembered can help us keep our priorities straight. It did for Alfred Nobel, who had the extraordinary opportunity to read his own obituary. It seems that after Alfred's brother died, a newspaper mistakenly printed Alfred's death notice. Though the article was positive, describing him as a brilliant chemist who made a great fortune as the inventor of dynamite, Nobel was horrified to be memorialized in such utilitarian terms.

Determined to leave a more positive legacy, he bequeathed his considerable wealth to the establishment of the Nobel Prizes.

TAKING ACTION

1. If you removed material items, career achievements, and recreational goals from your goals in life, what would be left?

_____

_____

_____

2. What are you looking to accomplish in the areas of:

   character maturity?

_____

_____

_____

   competence development?

_____

_____

_____

   impact on people?

_____

_____

_____

   family?

_____

_____

_____

3. Many companies hire consulting firms to complete long-term planning and examination. This process is considered essential to success. Play the role of a consultant and do some long-term planning for your life and priorities.

   Write a personal **Mission Statement**.

   What do you want to accomplish in life? Why do you exist?

   I exist to: _____

   _____

   _____

   _____

   Develop your personal **Core Values**.

What are the non-negotiables of your life?

_____

_____

_____

What things hold such a priority for you that you would defend these values at a great cost?

_____

_____

_____

Personal Core Values

1.

2.

3.

4.

5.

6.

7.

The Power of One means focusing on the right priorities; the wrong ones—or none at all—put the golden touch in jeopardy.

A California industrialist addressed a group of executives at a leadership seminar some time ago . . . He offered a lot of helpful advice, but one concept in particular has stuck in my head: "There are two things that are the most difficult to get people to do: to think, and do things in the order of their importance." —Charles Swindoll

---

Day 23

ASK OTHERS TO HOLD YOU ACCOUNTABLE FOR YOUR ACTIONS

As iron sharpens iron, so one man sharpens another.
—PROVERBS 27:17 NIV

DRIVING THOUGHT

The Power of One understands that leaning on others for an outside perspective can keep us out of the ditch.

DRILLING DOWN

No one was asking John Rigas any questions, and he wasn't looking for any questions to be asked. He was enjoying a life of complete independence, and all things were going his way. Or so he thought.

Rigas was an elder statesman of the business community and a generous public benefactor of Coudersport, Pennsylvania. This World War II veteran founded a small cable television company with his brother, and they managed to build it into a national corporation. Rigas prided himself on keeping the business local and family run—something his community and the local media loved to highlight.

He and his brother even named the company Adelphia, from the Greek word for *brother,* to symbolize his commitment to family and customer service. Rigas's strong business sense earned him the 1998 entrepreneur of the year by his alma mater, and the *Buffalo News* named him the city's most powerful and influential business leader in 2001. He was also a member of the Rotary Club and served on numerous boards.

All sounded well and good, but appearances were deceiving. In 2002 the real John Rigas started to show through the cracks. In May he resigned as chairman of Adelphia. In June his company filed bankruptcy. In July federal agents arrested him and his two sons for conspiracy. Rigas was accused of having used company money to buy the Buffalo Sabres hockey team, a golf course, real estate, and private jets, and hiding $2.3 billion in liabilities from investors. The total loss to the company he'd so lovingly built: $60 billion.

Rigas joined the corporate scandal world of Enron, Arthur Andersen, ImClone, and WorldCom, to name just a few. He lost personal integrity; his family-friendly, honest, and down-home style was shattered.[1]

He wasn't what he seemed. He hid his real self well—too well, in fact. Just think how things would have turned out differently had Rigas spoken with trusted advisors, honest family members, or a loving wife, about his plans before taking action. Had he talked more about his choices—before he made them—someone could have, most likely would have, steered him back on track. It's highly unlikely that numerous people would lead Rigas, the "family man," down the wrong road. But without their input and counsel, that's what happened.

Asking others to hold you accountable for your actions isn't a weak way to go; on the contrary. The more powerful you are in the business world, the more you need people to keep you on the straight and narrow. Being held accountable doesn't mean giving up autonomy or privacy. It means having an agreement with several trusted friends, colleagues, and advisors—people who are highly ethical—that they can check in with you from time to time and ask about your actions.

These people can simply ask, "Are you acting ethically in all that you do? Are you treating others with the golden rule—including your business?" Your answers, if honest, should be all that's needed to keep you trucking down the golden road of integrity.

SUMMARIZING PRINCIPLES

1. It is not a good thing for people to float through life answering only the scrutiny of their own review.

2. The best accountability has a runway in front and in back of the hard questions. That runway is mutual respect and deep acceptance.

3. Accountability only works if we let it work.

4. Good accountability thrives on penetrating questions from outsiders.

5. Effective accountability is like a Golden Safety Net.

MAKING EVALUATION

A paradigm shift has occurred in college football over the past decade. In years past, student athletes were released for the summer to return to their hometowns to work, reunite with friends and relatives, and to participate in a self-regulated preparation for the next season.

The test of a successful summer came in August when the players returned to school for two-a-day practices. Coaches tested their players to see who had worked hard during their summer break. Conditioning drills would be run over and over to weed out those who were obviously lazy while at home. Those who had put on too much weight or reported out of shape faced a blistering August.

Unfortunately, many failed the test each year. For some schools, those days are over now. In recognition of the difficulty of maintaining the self-discipline it takes to properly prepare for the season, coaching staffs are asking players to stay on campus and help each other reach their goals as a team. And guess what—it's working.

Players are entering the season better prepared, and the team is able to focus less on testing for conditioning and more on preparation for the season ahead. It's very simple to see why this shift has occurred; coaches recognize that when left unto ourselves, we are weak. Even a six-foot-seven-inch college football player with an NFL contract on the line finds it hard to have self-discipline to eat less and run more. The foundational concept at work is *accountability*. Athletes need it, and so do those who want to win in ethical behavior.

Has someone ever stood looking over your shoulder as you worked on a project or task? If so, chances are you didn't like it. Most people don't. And they like it even less when someone checks up on them to make sure they're being honest and responsible. Yet, that is what I'm suggesting you invite people to do if you want to live by the golden rule—because nothing helps to keep a person honest like accountability.

It's ironic. We don't like to be reminded of our shortcomings, and we don't like our shortcomings exposed to others either. But if we want to grow, we need to face the pain of exposing our actions to others. Integrity is the foundation of a person's life, and accountability is the cornerstone. It gives teeth to our pledge to live to high ethical standards.

We all need accountability, I guess. The other day, while visiting my accountant, his secretary mentioned that she needed to get a notary to sign off on a document from a priest for a piece of property she was selling. She commented that that was strange—to get a notary to back up the word of a priest. But, as she pointed out, we all need accountability, no matter our positions in life.

To make accountability work in your life, you need these things:

1. At least two people

It doesn't work for any of us to only be accountable to ourselves. We all have blind spots and areas in life in which we are stronger—and areas that we obviously need help with. It's not wise to ask for accountability in the areas you've got under control—and ignore the ones you struggle with. You need to do the reverse. Ask people to hold you accountable for those areas that you are vulnerable to.

Accountability works best when you have at least two people checking in on you. Why? You never see just one referee or umpire at a professional sporting event—there are always at least two, because each person brings a different perspective, level of experience, or view of the situation. Working together, these two people can give you the best advice and see your case more clearly.

The two people don't have to be best friends or lifetime mates. They can be older or younger and they can live in different locations. But accountability begins with someone outside yourself.

2. Proactive, penetrating questions

Accountability is built around questions. They can come through the front door or they can come through the back door—whether obvious and deliberate, or subtle and casual, but the key is that they have to come through some door. Invite your accountability partners to ask precise and hard-hitting questions that cause a pause in the conversation. You want them to ask the tough questions that make you think, and that sometimes cause you a little pain.

> *Conversation means being able to disagree and still continue the conversation.*
>
> — DWIGHT MACDONALD

Remember, a little pain now in questioning your activities and motives will save you enormous amounts of pain later when you've gone too far down the road to return.

3. The ability to listen

Accountability is not just the rapid firing of one question after the next. Yes, it's about asking questions, but it's also about listening. Encourage your accountability partners to leave you ample time after asking you questions to discuss your answers—and clarify any points that arise. You need them to truly care about you and your issues. They must take time to really get to know you, or else they'll never be able to pinpoint the right questions to ask.

4. Acceptance to know that if you fail, they will help you up

We all have failed, and we all will fail again. I love what Henry Beecher said: "Every man should have a fair-sized cemetery in which to bury the faults of his friends." The best kind of accountability is the kind that hopes for the best but deals with the worst. It doesn't create a standard of perfection that automatically means the accountability relationship is over if the standard is broken. There is a commitment, a safety net that both parties know is there to soften a fall and hopefully keep us ethically alive. A good accountability partner is very much a Golden Safety Net.

Nothing helps to keep a person honest like accountability.

1. Can you name any organizations or groups whose success is driven by accountability?

_____

_____

2. Have you experienced accountability at some level? For example, in dieting, exercising, in your marriage, or from your employer? What did accountability look like?

_____

_____

3. How did accountability help you achieve your goals?

_____

_____

4. Are you able to motivate and regulate yourself to achieve your goals? Grade yourself on self-discipline on a scale of 1 to 10, with 10 being the best: How disciplined are you?

_____

5. Can you identify an area of ethical behavior in which you need some accountability?

_____

Here's an example of accountability at work: An office administrator for a medium-sized organization told the story of a grueling three months of transition in which three of his four major department leaders resigned or transitioned to another place in the company. He was left to handle all of the production and on-ramping of new employees. His hours, stress level, and cell phone bill shot through the roof.

After the workload slowed some, this administrator felt as if he needed a day or two to recuperate, and that he deserved reimbursement for his enormous cell phone bill. The cell phone was a private account and the company had no history of giving comp days for excessive work demands. The administrator had the authority to order both for himself, but just to make sure it was on the up-and-up, he consulted two other leaders on the same level in the company. After gaining their assurance that both were good choices in light of the situation, he proceeded. He not only proceeded with the execution of the decisions, but he did so with a clear conscience and confidence gained through accountability.

Just be forewarned: Just because two people say it's OK to do something, know that you are ultimately responsible if the wrong choice is made. That means it's up to you to choose accountability partners whom you trust implicitly.

TAKING ACTION

There is strength in numbers. A piece of paper is easily torn in two, but it takes a pretty strong person to tear through all of the Atlanta phone book! Together we can resist tempting situations more easily, we can avoid poor decisions more easily, and we can maximize our potential when we live and work in the confines of a team atmosphere.

Ethics are maximized in the same manner. If we try to make ethical choices alone, we will rationalize and compromise our way into poor choices. To live out the golden rule, we need others to help. Consider forming an accountability group that gathers to encourage ethical behavior.

While a part of an accountability group, take these steps:

> *Two are better than one, because they have a good return for their work: If one falls down, his friend can help him up. But pity the man who falls and has no one to help him up! Though one may be overpowered, two can defend themselves. A cord of three strands is not quickly broken.*
>
> —KING SOLOMON

1. **Admit** you are weak and prone to fail if you try to live the golden rule alone.

   - Are you willing to tell others that you struggle?
   - How willing are you to share with others the deep things that linger in your thought life? Would you say you are very closed and need no help from others or totally an open book to everyone?

2. **Gather** others around you to help you succeed.
   - Who is in your Golden Safety Net?
   - For whom do you provide the Golden Safety Net?

3. **Meet** regularly to discuss your goals and struggles.

   - How often do you need others to ask you the tough questions? Once a month? Once a week? Daily? There's no right or wrong answer—just what works for you.

   _____

4. **Ask** your accountability partner/team to hold you accountable for three to five areas of ethical behavior.

   - Identify the five questions that, if asked regularly and answered honestly, could keep you in the middle of the ethical road.

   _____

   _____

   _____

   _____

   - What are the areas you want to change in living out the golden rule?

   _____

   _____

   _____

5. **Commit** to keeping the accountability issues confidential within your group.

   - How can you make accountability safe?

   _____

   _____

   _____

   _____

I don't want any yes-men around me. I want everyone to tell me the truth—even though it costs him his job. —Samuel Goldwyn

Day 24

Standing Up Without Always Standing Out

There is a point, of course, where a man must take the isolated peak and break with all his associates for clear principle; but until that time comes he must work, if he would be of use, with men as they are.

—Theodore Roosevelt

Driving Thought

The Power of One doesn't mean that I cause commotion or draw attention to myself in every stand for the good, the right, and the true.

Drilling Down

As a teenager, Dan hadn't traveled very far, and especially not far from home. And despite the fact that there was a war going on, Dan and his three childhood friends weren't too worried about their safety. Who would want to harm three teenage boys, anyway?

Apparently, someone did, because Dan and his friends were taken prisoner during the war. Many of the young boys his age were murdered.

Dan, however, was quickly identified as one of the gifted and talented few out of the prisoners. His captors put him to work. Soon he found the favor of his captors, but he still faced struggles during times of standing up for his beliefs and personal values.

This was how the story started. The story ends after Dan and his three buddies work for four different generations of leaders. Dan outlived three of his bosses, and outachieved their wildest expectations of his performance.

Who is this young man? He is the leader of the fearless foursome found in the Old Testament book named after him: Daniel. He worked under monarchy and he worked under democracy. He worked as an entry-level employee and he worked at the very top of the corporate ladder. He worked under people of different temperaments and belief systems. None of his leaders carried the same worldview or religious or political preferences that he did. Rulers died off one at a time, but young Daniel kept living and working, marking his life with character and competence.

For example, Daniel once worked as an upper-level overseer of 120 mid managers who were assigned the job of ruling over the affairs of the kingdom. The king needed someone to make sure his kingdom didn't "suffer loss." Because of Daniel's squeaky-clean image, he was put in charge. The king wanted to cut down on under-the-table payoffs. And Daniel did the job with utmost excellence.

> *Right is right, even if everyone is against it; and wrong is wrong, even if everyone is for it.*
>
> —WILLIAM PENN

I've never read or heard of anyone who has a more poster-perfect performance of how to stand up without always standing out. Young Daniel did it right, and it would be worth our noting his approach if we have any interest in standing up for our beliefs without always causing a three-alarm fire drill to go off.

It helps to remember Daniel's full story: He was a young Jew and had been asked to eat some food that wasn't approved for his diet, something of a religious and personal family tradition and belief. So what'd he do? We'll get to that, but let's look first at what he *didn't* do.

- He didn't dishonor himself or his superiors.

- He didn't say, "You idiots. Don't you know that I am a young Jew and I can't eat pork?"

- He didn't put his hands on his hips and, in disgust, huff and puff his way around the room.

- He didn't get mad, nor did he get defensive.

So what *did* he do?

- He carefully thought through the issue and tried to come up with a win-win alternative.

- He asked questions to clarify the situation and to gain more understanding.

- He used wisdom and tact when communicating with others.

- He worked through the proper channels. In other words, he didn't storm into the president's office and cause a scene. He simply worked the issue at the appropriate level.

SUMMARIZING PRINCIPLES

1. Standing up for the good, the right, and the true should always begin with modeling right actions.

2. Without a moral warehouse it is impossible to live a sustaining life of ethics.

3. Standing up doesn't have to be a bloodbath and bruises.

4. Living ethically doesn't mean that we have to be the self-appointed whistle-blower of all wrongs and indiscretions.

MAKING EVALUATION

Daniel easily could have blended in with his surroundings and gone along with everything his leaders asked him to do. But he had developed a warehouse of moral convictions, so he was able to make the right choices when he came to the ethical intersections of his life. A moral warehouse is an inventory bank that you have built in your own system, a clear understanding between right and wrong that helps guide your decisions. To build this warehouse you need to create a series of beliefs and convictions that are more deeply rooted than passing opinions. An opinion is something I hold, whereas a conviction is something that holds me.

Besides creating a moral warehouse, you also need to practice modeling your ethical behavior. As the saying goes, you have to walk the walk, not just talk the talk. A friend reminded me of the huge role that modeling plays in practicing the Power of One:

Be sure you put your feet in the right place, then stand firm.

— ABRAHAM LINCOLN

"As a parent I have learned that my children notice what I do more often than they hear what I say. For instance, I heard my wife correcting my daughter the other day about the way she put on her new shoes. It seems that she tied them once and then slipped them off only to shove her foot into them again without untying them. When her foot got stuck she just stomped really hard a few times until the back of the shoe buckled and caved inwards. My wife reminded her that she was ruining her brand-new shoes and to put them on properly. I didn't enter into the discussion.

"A few days later I was going to take my little girl somewhere and I slipped on my lace-up shoes. My daughter said, 'Dad I like to put my shoes on like you do, without untying them, but Mom won't let me.' She learned by watching me. I never sat her down to show her how to put on her shoes. She just picked it up from me. I was reminded of a valuable lesson: *More is caught than is taught!* I might even venture out to say that if I had tried to teach her this, she would have refused to do it."

More is caught than is taught. This is true in a home setting and it is true in a corporate setting. New employees tiptoe past the values that are posted on the company walls and begin operating with the same values that are modeled by the management of a company. More is caught than taught. That is irrefutable and sobering.

We can stand up for what we believe in without necessarily standing out in the crowd. Living ethically doesn't mean that we have to be the self-appointed whistle-blower of all wrongs and indiscretions but that we mark our commitment to the good, the right, and the true in appropriate and effective means. And it means that we don't have to grandstand on every moral issue—it's not about making a scene and making sure everyone knows we're doing the right thing. It's just about *doing* it; if others observe your right actions, all the better. The Power of One is maximized when the golden rule becomes who you really are and not just a choice you try to make.

> *Give us clear vision that we may know where to stand and what to stand for— because unless we stand for something, we shall fall for anything.*
>
> —PETER MARSHALL

Let me give you some guidelines to standing up without always standing out. Of course, you won't always be able to use these. Sometimes the ethical leak happens fast and unannounced and you have to perform an on-the-spot response with no time for thinking through the situation. However, most of the time you'll be able to work through this process to make the right decisions.

Think things through ahead of time.

A clear mind is critical to standing up for your convictions. Try your best to see the situation from as many angles as possible, and make sure there's really a moral violation taking place and not just a personal rub before speaking out.

I have a friend who uses one probing question to get to the bottom of ethical dilemmas: He asks the other party, usually in a business situation, what principles are driving them to make the decisions they're making—decisions that are often unethical and outright wrong. This allows my friend to gather data as well as learn the behind-the-scenes thoughts that prompted the other party to try to involve him in the situation at hand.

Remove the emotion.

Although emotions are helpful in many situations, now's not the time. Instead make your decision issues-oriented. Generally, when it comes to standing up for our beliefs, we've enveloped ourselves in a situation that is full of emotion. Doing so can also trigger us to say things that we really didn't mean to say or say things in the wrong way.

Another danger we may face is the danger of becoming fixed on the fight and losing the target. Many fighters lose the cause and get too involved in the notion of a good fight. Managing the emotions usually will help keep this problem in check.

Identify your approach to standing up.

How will you approach the situation? With a carefully worded letter or note? A one-on-one meeting with your boss or other involved parties? Will you make an announcement at the annual meeting? Or simply give the person a call? Different situations call for different responses. Analyze them carefully, and make sure you're directing your response to the right person. Don't call up the chief executive officer when a midlevel manager could solve the problem; conversely, don't fire off a letter to a store clerk who holds no power, when you'd be better off writing to the store owner or district manager.

> *It is often easier to fight for a principle than to live up to it.*
>
> —ADLAI STEVENSON

Solomon, in writing the book of Ecclesiastes, made a reference that most of us have heard, perhaps only at a funeral. He said there is a time for everything. He then went on to outline a list of life events that prove that. His point was that everything had its right time. In the matter of standing up without always standing out there is an appropriate time for different responses:

- A time to overlook
- A time to whisper
- A time to scream
- A time to confront
- A time to fight

Picking the right response is critical to getting your point across.

Talk it over with a friend.

Get a friend's angle on the issue and see whether you're thinking straight and seeing clearly. Ask for an honest response, a different perspective, from your friend, and consult several trusted advisors if it will help. We all have blind spots and need someone with a different vantage point to give us his or her thoughts and perspective.

Practice basic good manners.

In other words, don't scream and say things that really aren't relevant to the situation. Use appropriate speaking and listening skills. I will never forget a friend making a comment about a certain group of people. He said, "They are usually right in their orthodoxy; they are just so darn mean. I just don't like working with them. Let's go with someone else if possible."

Decide ahead of time what you're willing to lose.

Are you willing to lose your job? What about your short-term reputation? How about friends? Will you walk away from retirement and all the securities connected with that? Can you handle a heated, frank conversation? Decide up front what your convictions are worth to you, then stick to them.

The story is told that Henry Thoreau, a rugged New England individualist of the nineteenth century, once went to jail instead of paying his poll taxes to a state that supported slavery. Thoreau's good friend Ralph Waldo Emerson hurried to visit him in jail. Peering through the bars, he exclaimed, "Why Henry, what are you doing in there?" Thoreau replied, "Nay, Ralph, the question is what you are doing out there?

Anticipate the possible responses.

Don't overplay chess with this but it does help to spend a little time anticipating what kind of response you will get. Thinking through the enemy's response has always been a favorite strategic move in the battle. As one anonymous sage said, *"The enemies a person makes by taking a stand will have more respect for him than the friends he makes by being on the fence."*

> *I have found the greatest help in meeting any problems with decency and self-respect and whatever courage is demanded is to know where you yourself stand. That is, to have in words what you believe and are acting from.*
>
> —WILLIAM FAULKNER

Write out a script.

Crafting the problem and solution on paper will help bring precision and focus. Write out possible questions that you could use to help the conversation stay under control and on target.

Take your courage vitamin, pray, and make a stand.

If all signs point toward stand, then get up there and stand for your beliefs. Just make sure you've thought it through carefully and are ready to face come what may.

We need wisdom to sort and sift all the elements of life that come at us. Fred Holloman, former chaplain to the Kansas Senate, prayed one day at the opening of the session, "Omniscient Father, help us to know who is telling the truth. One side tells us one thing and the other side just the opposite. And if neither side is telling the truth, we would like to know that too. And if each is telling half the truth, give us the wisdom to put the right halves together."

TAKING ACTION

Standing up without always standing out involves at least three critical phases:

Embrace a set of convictions.

1. What is the difference between a conviction and an opinion?

2. Name one conviction that you have passionately embraced in regard to ethical behavior. Why is it so important to you?

3. Would you say that you have developed an adequate moral warehouse? What are some of your convictions?

4. Who would you say is your greatest role model of ethical behavior?

5. Name five qualities that you admire in this person:

_____

_____

_____

_____

_____

6. How much of this role model's influence has come through his or her direct teaching and speaking to you about ethics as opposed to his or her consistent modeling of ethical behavior?

        Teaching _____%   Modeling _____%

7. Why do actions speak so much louder than words?

_____

_____

_____

8. If we were to ask those who associate with you regularly, would they say that you are modeling ethical behavior? What are they catching from you?

_____

_____

_____

Filter life's choices through these convictions.

Our convictions are a set of lenses through which we view life. Our convictions red flag those things that violate our values and affirm those things that are in agreement.

Choose to act on your convictions

- when no one is watching
- consistently
- regardless of cost

- because it is right, not because others will hear about it
- because it is who you are

1. Do you struggle making consistent ethical choices?

_____

2. On a scale of 1 to 10, how strong are your convictions?

_____

3. What is your motivation for making ethical choices?

_____

_____

_____

4. If you make choices without others seeing them, why do they matter?

_____

_____

No one wants to be an echo, to live a shadow of a life. Yet that is often the fate of people without convictions. If you desire for your life to have meaning, then you must choose *some* principle to live by. So take the advice of nineteenth-century novelist George Eliot, who said, "Keep true, never be ashamed of doing right, decide on what you think is right and stick to it."

He who floats with the current, who does not guide himself according to higher principles, who has no ideal, no convictions—such a man is a mere article of the world's furniture—a thing moved, instead of a living and moving being—an echo, not a voice. —Henri Frederic Amiel

TREAT PEOPLE BETTER
THAN THEY TREAT YOU

We should ever conduct ourselves toward our enemy as if he were one day to be our friend.

—JOHN HENRY NEWMAN

DRIVING THOUGHT

The Power of One doesn't retaliate or get even.

DRILLING DOWN

We had been waiting for this scene and this moment for more than a half a year. Back in December of the previous year, we had met at Chili's, as we have every year for more than a decade, and planned the next trip.

This next year's trip was going to be a little different and a lot more special. We were going to fly into an outpost lake in Canada. The group was made up of the same last names, only this year's trip would include sons. Four of the dads wanted to bring their older boys and let them experience the North Woods and the incredible top-water action that small-mouth bass fishing provides.

We flew through Minneapolis and headed north. After landing in Winnipeg we shuttled by minivan to the base camp where we then caught our float plane and took the thirty-minute ride to the outpost lake. We were going to be the only fishermen on the entire lake. That was the plan and one of the big selling points of this outfitter.

You just have to like doing this kind of thing to even get close to the excitement. It was incredible. As the big otter rumbled through the Canadian skies, we finally saw it . . . our cabin. After eight months of planning and waiting, the moment had arrived.

The float plane pilot had said that we would be unloading first, and then the group coming out would load up and take off. We throttled to the pier after landing on the lake and then began to unload. All of our stuff was put on the dock and the departing party's stuff was quickly loaded and the otter took wings.

Alone. Just the eight of us: four dads and four sons.

The first thing to do was to get all the stuff safely into the cabin and then take off on the lake. Every guy who walked through the front door of the cabin caught the same snapshot. It was a garbage dump inside.

The guys who had just flown off left food on plates that were put back into the cabinets. They had left rotten food lying around. There was trash stacked on trash, and trash just circulating looking for a place to land. The place was sickening. When a group of outdoorsy teenage boys get sick because of the filth, you know it's bad.

> *Before you embark on a journey of revenge, dig two graves.*
> —CONFUCIUS

We cleaned it up, missed the first few hours of fishing, and then went on to have a spectacular week. At the end of a spectacular week of fishing, Uncle Alan led the clean-up crew. As we started, the obvious took place. One of the fellows asked, "Well, why are we going to clean this place up so well? The guys who left it for us did nothing."

Every dad lives for such a teaching moment. Uncle Alan grabbed it and poked it right out of the park, "Because it is the right thing to do. If all we do is what the last guys did, we are no better than them. Somebody has to break the badness cycle, and it might as well be us. So," Alan announced, "we are going to leave this cabin cleaner than it has ever been left."

The trip was a success in every way imaginable.

SUMMARIZING PRINCIPLES

1. The golden rule has no place for revenge.

2. Playing an eye for an eye hurts you more than it hurts others.

3. You'll never get ahead by pushing others behind.

4. Learn to become a blesser to others instead of getting even when you are harmed.

MAKING EVALUATION

You can develop a Midas touch *with people* by taking your focus off of yourself and what you can gain, and instead focusing on adding value to others. It's easy to love people who love you. And showing kindness to people who treat you well is little more than common courtesy. But how do you respond to poor treatment from others? Do you return disrespect with disrespect? Do you meet aggression with aggression? It doesn't take much for unkindness to escalate into greater conflict. Take a look at some of these seemingly petty disagreements that grew into full-blown war:

- A dispute over a well bucket, about nine hundred years ago between the cities of Modena and Bologna, began a war that devastated Europe.

- A Chinese emperor once went to war over the breaking of a teapot.

- Sweden and Poland flew at each other's throats in 1654 because the king of Sweden discovered that his name in an official dispatch was followed by only two *et ceteras*, while the king of Poland had three.

- The spilling of a glass of water on the Marquis de Torey led to war between France and England.

- By throwing a pebble at the Duc de Guise, a small boy caused the massacre of Vassy and the Thirty Years' War.

It takes a person of strong character to treat others better than they treat you. As civil rights leader Martin Luther King Jr. said, *"Forgiveness is not an occasional act; it is a permanent attitude."* If everyone practiced the golden rule, the world would be a better place. But think about what kind of world it would be if everyone strove to treat others *better* than they are treated. I call that living by the *platinum* rule.

I believe there is a wealth greater than money, and it comes from how you interact with others. It takes a person of strong character to treat others better than they treat you! If there ever is a time that the golden ruler is needed, it is when you need to return a better action than you were given. This can be done by refocusing on:

1. What is good

2. What is right

3. What is true

How do you react when someone mistreats you? Whether it is a big offense or a small matter of contention, we all must deal with the malice others show toward us. Which of the following is your natural mode of operation?

- **The Avenger.** This hero of revenge lives by the "eye for an eye" principle. This person returns a verbal jab for a verbal jab. When he is pushed, he pushes back. He keeps a record of rights and wrongs and makes sure everyone is even.

- **The Avoider.** This mode of operation is a little more subtle. There is no outward sign of revenge, but internally this person cuts the offending party off. Bitterness develops inside his or her heart. It is an internal termination. "If you mistreat me, then I'll just cut you out of my routine. You will receive a smile, but in my heart you are long gone." The avoidance is an attempt to avert further mistreatment. The avoidance is also an attempt to prevent having to ever help the mistreated.

- **The Taker.** This person does nothing. He or she views mistreatment as the way it is. Imagine a punching bag. The role of the bag is to receive abuse and never do anything about it.

- **The Blesser.** This way of reacting to mistreatment is rare. This person actually returns kindness for mistreatment. The goal is to treat others well no matter how they treat you. Think of Jesus, who was nailed to a cross, all the while praying for the forgiveness of his murderers.

1. Which of the above best describes your normal mode of operation when someone mistreats you?

     The Avenger   The Avoider   The Taker   The Blesser

2. Which one displays the most strength? Why?

_____

_____

3. Which one displays the Golden Touch?

4. Why is the concept of being "The Blesser" or treating others better than they treat you so strange?

_____

_____

5. How can being "The Blesser" benefit the situation?

_____

_____

_____

TAKING ACTION

Treating others better than they treat you is next-level thinking. It is taking the golden rule to the extreme. There was an ancient king who lived out this kind of next-level thinking. King David, the second king of Israel, assumed the throne after a battle with King Saul that lasted several years. It was the custom of the day to kill off all of the former king's relatives and allies upon assuming the throne to prevent any future claim or battle for power. Upon David's ascension to power, Saul's relatives were destroyed.

All except one: Mephibosheth. He was lame in both feet and had nothing to offer David. In fact, he had a claim to David's throne as the only surviving relative of the former king. Mephibosheth was actually King David's enemy, but King David chose not to kill him, nor did he enslave or imprison him. David instead restored to Mephibosheth all of his family's land. He gave him a place in the palace and a seat at the royal table for the rest of his days (2 Samuel 9).

King David understood next-level thinking. He was fleshing out treating others better than they deserve to be treated. He exhibited the Power of One.

How can we begin to grasp this kind of perspective? How can we begin to live out next-level thinking? Two words will lead us: *give up*. That's right, your eyes are not fooling you. Giving up is the key.

GIVE UP!

Give up the ledger.

Quit keeping a record of rights and wrongs! Shut down the accounting department. Erase any debts you feel others owe you because of their mistreatment. Shift to a new basis for your treatment of others. Treat them well regardless of how they treat you.

Give up the "antiwimp" perspective.

Let go of your fear of being viewed as soft. Let go of the thought that you are a wimp if you don't repay every wrong. It actually takes more strength to treat others well in the face of mistreatment.

There is an ancient proverb that says, "If your enemy is hungry, give him food to eat; if he is thirsty, give him water to drink. In doing this, you will heap burning coals on his head." The stronger person is the one who shows kindness to those who mistreat him.

Give up your competitive nature.

Many of us hate to lose more than anything in the world. Whether it is Little League or racquetball, we are competitive to the core. To allow someone to one-up us in the office or in a relationship would be conceding a loss. That is un-American! Exhibiting the Golden Touch is not a game. Remember that treating others better than they treat you is a win.

Give up your rights.

We all believe that we have the right to be treated fairly. The customer is always right. Faster drivers get the left lane. If your pizza arrives in more than thirty minutes, then it's free. But in order to live out next-level thinking, we have to give some rights up. We can't treat others better than they treat us if we are demanding justice and fairness. By giving up those rights, we are laying the foundation for next-level living.

> *Sometimes we find it hard to forgive. We forget that forgiveness is as much for us as for the other person. If you can't forgive it's like holding a hot coal in your hand—you're the one getting burned.*
>
> —JENNIFER JAMES

- Why is "giving up" such a hard concept to embrace?

_____

_____

_____

- How can "giving up" bring freedom to your life?

_____

_____

_____

- How do you think Mephibosheth's life was impacted by King David's "giving up"?

_____

_____

_____

Name a mistreatment you have experienced.	How do you feel when wronged?	How can you live out treating them better?

You have to get beyond blaming others . . . give up your excuses . . .
—Price Pritchett, Ph.D.

Day 26

WALK THE SECOND MILE

Walk a mile in my shoes, walk a mile in my shoes
Yeah, before you abuse, criticize and accuse,
Walk a mile in my shoes.

—JOE SOUTH AND THE BELIEVERS

DRIVING THOUGHT

The Power of One delivers over and above the expected and the assumed.

DRILLING DOWN

In October 2001, Felix Del Valle Senior was diagnosed with amyotrophic lateral sclerosis (ALS), or Lou Gehrig's disease. ALS attacked Felix's nerve cells and pathways in his brain and spinal cord. As his cells deteriorated, he began to lose voluntary muscle control and the ability to move. His first concern, as a single parent, was not about the disease that would take his life, but for the future of his four children.

Lori Burgess, an administrator with the Visiting Nurse Association, had known Felix simply as the sandwich maker in her office cafeteria—the guy who lit up lunch hour with his smile.[1] When she heard he was sick, she went to speak to him.

"He was more worried about his kids than about himself," Burgess recalled. "It occurred to me ten minutes later that my husband and I could take them in with our three kids." When she told her family of Felix's plight, her husband David didn't hesitate. Neither did the three Burgess children. "What if it were us?" David Jr. asked. It was as simple as that.[2]

Felix was buried just before Father's Day, 2003. The Del Valle family is learning to live their lives without their father. The Burgess family is learning to live their lives with four new members. All are learning to understand the golden rule.

That's going the second mile.

What about walking the first mile? you might ask. Going the first mile would have been giving sympathy and concern, maybe sending a flower arrangement or allocating some money for college funding. Would that have been helpful? You bet it would have been. The Del Valles would have appreciated the gesture. But the Burgess family went one mile further. And those extra steps—huge steps—made all the difference in the lives of those kids.

SUMMARIZING PRINCIPLES

1. Going the second mile usually requires taking a step of risk.
2. Going the second mile activates a bond of care and concern that is hard to break between people.
3. Going the second mile is more about will than it is wisdom.
4. Going the second mile usually catches people by surprise.
5. Going the second mile evokes a strong response from those on the receiving end—and the end of the givers.

MAKING EVALUATION

Two millennia ago in the Roman Empire, a Roman officer could compel anyone to carry a load one mile. It was the officer's right, and a person refused at his peril. So to walk the first mile was to do what was required. I'm recommending you not only do that, but strive to go above and beyond that. See the extra mile as an opportunity to make a positive impact on the lives of others, to add value to people.

A person with an extra-mile attitude is someone who:

> Cares more than others think is wise
> Risks more than others think is safe
> Dreams more than others think is practical
> Expects more than others think is possible
> Works more than others think is necessary

As my friend Zig Ziglar says, "There's no traffic jam on the extra mile." If you always do more than is expected, not only will you rise up above the crowd; you will help others to rise up with you.

A friend recounted a trip he and his wife had just returned from. They had driven from Mobile, Alabama, to West Texas to visit the widow of a college buddy who had suddenly died. He and his wife felt that they needed to go check on his friend's widow.

During the visit my friend discovered that the widow had no insurance and had been left with very little money. So my friend walked the second mile. He arranged to have her whole financial world evaluated, and in the meantime he paid for her insurance ahead for the next year. He still calls her every week to check on her.

She asked as he was leaving, "Why would you go to all the trouble and sacrifice to do this for me?" My friend responded, "Because your husband would have wanted me to. Because you are family. And because it is the right thing to do. It is what I would want someone to do for my wife if I died suddenly."

> *Kindness is a language the dumb can speak and the deaf can hear and understand.*
>
> —CHRISTIAN BOVEE

The road of the second mile is sometimes a road that demands a few things extra from us. It's not easy on us. It's often time-consuming, expensive, and tiresome. But that's why it's called the "extra" mile.

1. A person with an extra-mile attitude is someone who *cares more than others think is wise*.

It is a very old saying, but it is still as profound as the first time it was uttered. And it will be true until there is no one else walking on the earth. *People don't care how much you know until they know how much you care.*

Do you truly care . . .

about those around you?

about your organization?

about yourself?

2. A person with an extra-mile attitude is someone who *risks more than others think is safe*.

On a scale of 1 to 10, what level of risk are you willing to live by to go the second mile?

_____ Personal Life

_____ Work Life

_____ Community Life

3. A person with an extra-mile attitude is someone who *dreams more than others think is practical*.

Which is a bigger influence on your behavior: dreams or practicality? Why?

_____

_____

_____

4. A person with an extra-mile attitude is someone who *expects more than others think is possible*.

   Are you an optimist or a pessimist? Why?

_____

_____

_____

5. A person with an extra-mile attitude is someone who *works more than others think is necessary*.

   What is your determining factor for knowing you have done well at work?

6. Why should we go the second mile?

_____

_____

_____

Imagine yourself in the place of another person. Simply ask, "How would I like to be treated in this situation?" Understanding the golden rule helps you identify who might be affected and how they might be impacted by the actions you choose to take.

One of the wonderful things about the golden rule is that it makes the intangible tangible. You don't need to know the law. You don't need to explore nuances of philosophy. You simply imagine yourself in the place of another person. Even a small child can get a handle on that. There are no complicated rules or loopholes.

> *Doing my best at this present moment puts me in the best place for the next moment.*
>
> —OPRAH WINFREY

No complicated rules. No loopholes. No secrets. Simple as that! A genuine consideration of others is essential to an ethical life.

TAKING ACTION

1. Whose shoes have you walked in lately? What was that person's story? What did you learn?

_____

_____

_____

_____

_____

_____

_____

2. Who has walked in yours? Why?

_____

_____

_____

3. Let's get really practical. Going the second mile is about surpassing the industry standard. It is about exceeding expectations, and it's very rare. Reflect on walking the second mile in the following five areas of life. Name an expectation within the area and then think of a way to go beyond that standard.

Life Area	Standard Expectations	Second-Mile Idea
Work		
Personal Health		
Family		
Community Service		
Finances		

A. How would others' views of you change if you implemented second-mile living?

_____

_____

_____

_____

B. Who would benefit from your second-mile actions?

_____

_____

_____

_____

C. What is your biggest obstacle to walking the second mile?

_____

_____

_____

_____

Africa was the last populated continent to be explored and penetrated by the British or any Europeans. It was called the "Dark Continent" because it was shrouded in mystery. No one knew what its vast interior held, or what might be found there. The mosquito-infested coast and disease-ridden swamps and jungles barred any European from probing further. When Scottish missionary Mungo Park tried to lead an expedition up the Niger in 1805, every European on the trip died. Two-thirds of the British soldiers who landed on the African coast between 1823 and 1827 died of diseases ranging from malaria and dysentery to sleeping sickness and yellow fever. In 1824 alone, 221 out of 224 perished. Africa truly was "the white man's graveyard."

One man opened up Africa, and did that, not to enrich himself or to plant the flag of his country on another shore, but to bring Africans medicine, education, and freedom from slavery. David Livingstone was born to a very poor Scottish family outside Glasgow in 1818. He grew up in a one-room tenement. His father was a traveling tea salesman. He worked fourteen-hour days in a textile factory, then went to school at night. He wrote years later, "I resolved to devote my life to the alleviation of misery, both as a missionary and as a doctor."

In 1838 he had his medical degree, and as he was making plans to go to China as a missionary, he met a man named Robert Moffat who gave a lecture in Glasgow on the mission he had just opened in southern Africa. As Moffat told his audience of the vastness of the African continent and its unexplored beauty, or rising in the morning to see the smoke of a thousand villages where no missionary had been before, the image stuck in Livingstone's mind. He set sail from Liverpool on December 8, 1840, hardly dreaming he would not see home again for sixteen years.

Over the next three decades, Livingstone explored and mapped the continent of Africa from one side to the other. He brought medical help to thousands of villages. He became an international celebrity, the most famous explorer of his day, which was an era of exploration. At one time he had been gone so long that the world thought he was dead. A journalist named Henry Stanley journeyed over two years to find him, and thus the famous introduction between the two of them when Stanley walked up to him in a village and said: "Dr. Livingstone, I presume." Livingstone's health had finally given out. For months he had lain on a cot, too ill to move or lift a pen. But he refused to leave Africa. Instead, he said farewell to Stanley and set off on his final journey into the interior. On May 1, 1873, Livingstone died. His two constant companions, Chuma and Susi, former freed slaves, found his body kneeling at the foot of his cot, as he was about to say his prayers. They wrapped his body in calico to try to preserve it, and set off on an incredible eleven-month, fifteen-hundred-mile journey to the coast so that his body could be buried in England. It was a labor of love and a tribute to Livingstone from the people he had tried to protect and serve.

> *The value of compassion cannot be over-emphasized ... No greater burden can be borne by an individual than to know no one cares or understands.*
>
> —ARTHUR H. STAINBACK

David Livingstone spent thirty-two years in Africa. His wife and one of his children died in Africa. He traveled more than forty thousand miles.

London is a city full of statues, statues of kings and queens and of Winston Churchill and Admiral Lord Nelson. I'm not much for looking at statues, but I really do like the one of David Livingstone that is displayed prominently outside the prestigious Royal Geographic Society. He is buried at Westminster Abbey. On the tomb is inscribed: DAVID LIVINGSTONE: MISSIONARY, TRAVELER, PHILANTHROPIST.

Few people will spend their lives on another continent working on behalf of all of mankind. However, every one of us will wake up every day and be put in situations in which we can do the extraordinary. If we choose to walk the second mile with the situations that come into our lives, we will be practicing the Power of One with all the flare of David Livingstone.

Do a David Livingstone. Better yet . . . do a Lori Burgess.

Go the second mile with someone right there in your own backyard.

You can start right where you stand and apply the habit of going the extra mile by rendering more service and better service than you are now being paid for. —Napoleon Hill

Day 27

HELP PEOPLE WHO CAN'T HELP YOU

You have not lived today successfully unless you've done something for someone who can never repay you.

— JOHN BUNYAN

DRIVING THOUGHT

The Power of One helps others simply because it is the good, the right, and the true thing to do, without any thought of reciprocation.

DRILLING DOWN

For some reason, when we think of helping others, many of us think of doing so on a large scale. At Christmastime, we might donate canned food to a food pantry to help numerous people. Or we donate large sums of money to feed, clothe, or educate those who are less fortunate. And those are great things to do. But part of the Power of One is remembering that *one* person can make a difference for another *one* person.

What I'm saying is, don't dismiss helping others because you'll only be serving one or a small handful of people—that's often where you can make the biggest impact. And, this is a big *and*, do for others without expecting anything in return. Seriously. Take a page from Dan Cathy's book:

Dan Cathy, president of Chic-Fil-A, was invited to speak at a business luncheon in northwest Arkansas. As any good executive does, he also scheduled some time with the managers and employees of the local Chick-Fil-A stores in the area.

Soon, with the help of Jim, one of the local store owner/operators, Dan's schedule was filled to the brim. One meeting that stood out was a chance to speak to a large gathering of college students at the University of Arkansas. A representative of the school's fraternities and sororities assured Dan that there was plenty of interest, so they booked one of the school's largest ballrooms, set up a powerful sound system, and ordered books to pass out to all of the students in attendance. Obviously, they were expecting a crowd.

What they got, however, were four students. That's it, just four. Not four thousand, four hundred, or even forty, but four. But Dan took it in stride. He could have canceled, saying it wasn't worth his time to speak to such a small crowd. He could have charged for lost opportunity. But instead, Dan pulled up four chairs and asked the students to have a seat.

The four men got personal attention from one of the family members and leaders of one of the world's largest privately held companies. They were expecting a free seminar and to be one of hundreds in attendance. What they got was worth a semester's college education. Dan asked each man in attendance to tell his story—what's going on in his life, what are his goals, what does life have in store. The men opened up and shared from their hearts.

What did Dan do next? Just nod, say "good to hear it," and get on the road? Of course not. Dan asked if he could say a prayer for each of the men, and they all accepted.

These four men got a great experience—a night of talking to an experienced businessman who's also a kind and generous soul. And what did Dan get in return? Nothing. Nothing but the knowledge that he made a difference in the lives of others, when he could just have easily passed on the whole thing.

Dan will likely never know what kind of impact his time had on these students. But he'll always know he spent time with others—and expected nothing in return. Ironically, that's the greatest "reward" one could ever hope for.

SUMMARIZING PRINCIPLES

1. Helping people who could never help us in return signifies the purest of motives.

2. The spirit of reciprocation fuels much of our actions of benevolence and generosity.

3. An unquenchable joy accompanies anyone who develops the habit of helping others who can never pay them back.

4. We all have what it takes to start giving generously now.

MAKING EVALUATION

Let's face it: We don't often think like writer John Bunyan, who said, "You have not lived today successfully unless you've done something for someone who can never repay you." Yet if we want to live at the highest level, that's what we must do.

One of my favorite examples of that kind of help occurred during the Winter Olympics in 1964. Back then, the greatest bobsledder of all time, Italy's Eugenio Monti, was engaged in the two-man bobsled competition. The Italians made good time during their first run. So did the British team, with driver Tony Nash in charge. Following Monti's second run, he was in first place. And it looked as if he and his teammate might win the gold medal as long as the Brits didn't surpass them.

As the British team prepared for their second and final run, they made a demoralizing discovery. During the first run, a bolt had broken on their rear axle, and they didn't have a replacement. They had no choice but to drop out. But Eugenio Monti, who was waiting at the bottom of the hill to see if his time would hold up, heard about what had happened to the British team. He removed a bolt from the rear axle of his own sled and sent it up the hill to his competitor. Nash's team used the bolt, made their run, and won the gold medal. Monti and his teammate ultimately finished in third place.

There was no way that Nash could repay Monti. And there was no way Monti could benefit from giving Nash the bolt. Yet he did it anyway. The criticism against him in the Italian press was scathing. But he let everyone know that he wanted to win only if he truly was the best. "Tony Nash did not win because I gave him a bolt," explained Nash. "Tony Nash won because he was the best driver."[1]

Doing something for someone who can never repay you is a good thing. It's a way of "cleaning out your system," if you will. We have all kinds of toxins in our system—I'm talking about the soul toxins, not the other kinds. One such toxin is the way we treat others and the way we expect others to repay our kindness and actions. That is called reciprocation.

Reciprocation is the return of a favor. Most of us treat our spouses, our friends, and our companies with a "you scratch my back and I'll scratch yours" attitude. We lead with the question, What's in it for me?

> *The best index to a person's character is (a) how he treats people who can't do him any good, and (b) how he treats people who can't fight back.*
>
> —ABIGAIL VAN BUREN

How much of your treatment toward others is really a selling job? You are doing something so that it can be registered and somehow make its way back to you when you need it the most.

That is certainly how most of us live. And then when someone comes along who helps others who can never repay them, it is so fresh and pure.

The Power of One person practicing the golden rule pushes us past this shallow way of thinking. We all like to be given to or served without an expectation of repayment. So we should in turn live the same way.

1. Are you a giving person? Name three ways you regularly give of your time and resources:

a.

b.

c.

2. If a person is measured not by what they have, but what they give, how do you measure up?

_____ I keep it all

_____ I keep a lot and give a little

_____ I give a lot and keep a little

_____ I am a very generous giver

3. Why do we struggle with helping others?

_____

_____

_____

4. What is the benefit of helping someone who cannot give anything in return?

_____

_____

_____

5. Many people speak of the "joy" they find in serving and giving of themselves and their resources. Can you identify with this joy? Describe it.

_____

_____

_____

TAKING ACTION

Living the Power of One on this topic could be dangerous. Be careful; you might just help someone out and in the process find a little joy for yourself.

Spend some time working through the following action steps:

Think of a face.

Can you think of someone you regularly cross paths with who could use some help, but could never repay you? What is one way you could help this person? List specific steps—then take action!

_____

_____

_____

_____

_____

Audit your schedule.

Can you find one hour in the week to donate to a cause in your community? Brown-bag a lunch one day a week and donate your lunch hour to those in need. When and how could you serve an organization in your community?

_____

_____

_____

Clean your closet.

Can you think of five things sitting around your house or garage that you haven't touched in six months that you could donate to meet a need? What are they? Who can you give them to and when can you do that?

_____

_____

_____

_____

Adjust your budget.

Can you budget a certain percentage of your income solely for giving to others? Start somewhere and increase it half a percentage point every year. Use the money to meet needs as they arise in your context. What percent could you begin with today?

Anne Sullivan grew up in abject poverty. She and her brother were actually sent to a poorhouse to live, which is where her brother died. Anne suffered from an eye disease that made it very difficult to see. In fact, she was legally blind before one of many surgeries improved her sight.

When the poorhouse was shut down after a Massachusetts state investigation, Sullivan was accepted to the Perkins School for the Blind in Boston. There she flourished, and years later she was referred by the school to tutor a young girl named Helen Keller, who was blind and deaf.

Sullivan moved from Boston to Alabama to live with the Kellers; the transition was rough. No one could communicate with Helen, who was out of control as a child. Anne simply worked with Helen patiently—long after others would have given up and left town in tears and disgust.

But finally that patience paid off and the light dawned on Helen Keller: the finger motions Anne Sullivan was making in Helen's hand were a form of communication, not just random touching. A remarkable education and a strong relationship began.[2]

Anne Sullivan was a giver, not a taker. She practiced the Power of One. She gave to others and never had the first notion that it could or would benefit her—and her time made all the difference in the life of Helen Keller and her family.

What kind of difference have you made recently? What kind of difference do you plan to make? Don't just plan for it—do it!

All that this world knows of living lies in giving—and more giving.
He that keeps, be sure he loses. Friendship grows by what it uses.
—Alexander Maclaren

Day 28

Do Right When It's Natural to Do Wrong

Always do right. This will gratify some people and astonish the rest.

—MARK TWAIN

DRIVING THOUGHT

The Power of One means that regardless of personal cost or strength of opposition, I continue to pursue what is right—both for me and for others.

DRILLING DOWN

In a moment of private decision, Boris Kornfeld decided that he would not obey any inhumane orders or prison camp rules—even if doing so would cause him to lose his life. The Russian doctor, who was a prisoner in a Siberian gulag, had been treating a guard who had been injured. In that process he had actually considered taking surgical action that would have killed the guard. Those guards, after all, were his tormentors.

Kornfeld was shocked by his own thoughts that day, and so made a quiet commitment to himself. He had been studying The Lord's Prayer, a copy of which he had received from another prisoner. The simple prayer had caused a profound God-change to take place in his thinking and his life. In this place of cruelty, he would be different. He would do right. He would not turn a blind eye to injustice. He would practice the golden rule.

Soon after, Kornfeld saw a fellow prisoner stealing bread from a sick patient in the hospital. Without food, the patient would die. Kornfeld informed the guards of the infraction, even though he knew that by doing so he would be targeted by the prisoner who had stolen the bread. To protect himself, Kornfeld began to sleep in the hospital where there was a greater measure of protection.

Sometime later, a patient was admitted to the hospital. This seriously ill prisoner had stomach cancer, and as Kornfeld treated him, he decided to share the transformation that had taken place in his life. Kornfeld spoke at length; the prisoner listened with little response. He heard what the doctor was saying but had too little energy to process the information.

That night, the prisoner on whom Kornfeld had informed killed him brutally. The sick patient recovered and, as a result of Kornfeld's personal story, experienced a conversion of his own. He, Alexander Solzhenitsyn, then told the story. That story—along with many others— eventually earned him a Nobel prize.[1]

It would have been so much easier for Boris Kornfeld to go on his way and stay out of the fray. Stepping up and doing the good, the right, and the true isn't always our first reflex. And it's far from easy, most of the time. But by choosing the narrow gate of good, we bring honor to life and many times make an investment in eternity. Boris did just that. And it happened because he chose the Golden Path of Goodness: He did right when it was natural to do wrong.

SUMMARIZING PRINCIPLES

1. Stepping up and doing the good, the right, and the true isn't always our first reflex.

2. Many of us have been programmed toward choosing the wrong thing and reacting the wrong way.

3. Wrong sometimes seems, feels, and is easier at the outset.

4. It is possible to grow our ethical muscles so that the good, the right, and the true become the first move.

MAKING EVALUATION

When shopping, it's often not the price of an item that's a concern—it's the perceived value of the item versus the price that people focus on more. Don't believe me? Think about this: When you're shopping for groceries, you probably look for the best bargains on items your family eats for lunches. For many, lunches are just the things that fill you up until dinner, so you don't eat elaborately and you don't pay much, either. On the other hand, when you and your spouse are celebrating an anniversary, money is no object—you willingly fork over twenty dollars or more for a tiny appetizer, something you wouldn't have paid for your weekday lunch. It's all about value—at the restaurant you're getting service, ambience, convenience, and time with people who are important to you. At lunch, you're just getting food.

When dealing with ethics, people often think about how much they'll have to "pay" to do what is good, right, and true. Being honest with the cashier who gave you too much change means losing the extra $7.50—but it means keeping your reputation as a good and honest person. Not cooking the books to meet sales numbers will "cost" you a promotion, a bonus, or a salary raise. Is it worth it to you? Better yet, if you get caught, will having cooked the books have been worth it still? It's all about value—what you value in life and what you're willing to pay to get it.

Ethics are about how we meet the challenge of doing the right thing when that will cost more than we want to pay. Most deeds born out of the good, the right, and the true come with a price and require a resoluteness that must summon up depth of character.

Simply put, it's easier to do wrong sometimes. It takes less effort, seemingly gets you further ahead in life, and is sometimes just more fun. Why do other businesspeople do wrong? Here's their list:

- It's easier to do wrong sometimes because the crowd is moving with you and doesn't demand that you swim upstream.

- It's easier to do wrong sometimes because there are no immediate negative consequences.

- It's easier to do wrong sometimes because it just feels better.

- It's easier to do wrong sometimes because the violation just isn't that big of a deal—to you, at least.

Are those reasons good enough for you? What if you got caught? Remember, a strong backbone in moments of ethical temptation will save you from endless pain later on.

Peggy Noonan spent quite some time writing speeches for former president Ronald Reagan. Since then she has written a lot of articles sharing the mind and heart of Reagan. In thinking of Reagan's approach to world peace and handling other world leaders, she said, "When you're strong, you can be 'weak.' When you know you are strong, you can trust yourself to make the first move, the first appeal, a request or a plea. . . . But when you fear you are weak or fear the world thinks you are weak, you are more inclined to make a great show of being 'strong,' and never write a personal letter asking for peace."[2]

> I care not what others think of what I do, but I care very much about what I think I do: That is character!
>
> —THEODORE ROOSEVELT

1. Why do you think it's easier to do wrong—rather than stand up for what's right—in your own life?

2. List three situations in which you failed to stand up for the good, the right, and the true. What consequences did you endure as a result?

3. Now list three situations in which you took the ethical highroad. What made you do the right thing then—and how did it feel afterward?

A few years ago you might have seen the feature *You Make the Call* that was run during National Football League games. Each episode showcased a difficult or complex situation during a game in which an official had to make a ruling. The feature asked the TV audience to take a position on what the referee's decision should have been.

Upon returning from commercial, the feature would end by showing the right decision being made on the field by the referee, backed by an explanation from the rule book. The NFL has a standard to use in making calls on the field.

> *If you would convince a man that he does wrong, do right. Men will believe what they see.*
>
> —HENRY DAVID THOREAU

In light of our golden-rule standard, and our commitment to practice the Power of One, let's play . . . You Make the Call!

Was the call right or wrong in the following situations?

Golden Challenge #1 – Right Wrong – On a recent business trip, a person took out some personal friends and paid for it with the corporate credit card and called it a "business dinner."

Golden Challenge #2 – Right Wrong – A sales associate alters the numbers on a product just a little to make it sound great, while knocking down his competitor's product to make it sound like a bad deal.

Golden Challenge #3 – Right Wrong – A job applicant beefs up his or her résumé by adding a few false titles held at previous jobs, and even adds a few grade points to his college GPA.

Golden Challenge #4 – Right Wrong – A person takes a five-hundred-sheet ream of paper home because he or she occasionally does some printing for work on the home computer.

Golden Challenge #5 – Right Wrong – A person uses the company phone to make personal long distance calls while on the clock.

If you chose "wrong" on all of the questions, then congratulations. You made the right call! Why are these things easily seen as wrong, yet many people—maybe yourself included—do them regularly?

_____

_____

_____

What should be your ultimate motivation for choosing to do right?

_____

_____

_____

Ultimately doing right will pay off. Explain this outcome.

_____

_____

_____

TAKING ACTION

The Power of One is definitely put to the test as we choose right over wrong each day. Ultimately, the test of true character is what we do when no one is watching.

1. Is there an area of your life that you would change upon finding out that your boss was watching you?
2. Can you think of a situation in which you chose to do wrong and didn't get caught?
3. Would you like someone to make this choice at your expense?
4. How can you prevent yourself from making that same choice again if given the opportunity?

_____

_____

_____

5. Can you identify the pressure points that cause you to feel the temptation to make wrong choices?

_____

_____

_____

6. Who in your life is a model of making choices with integrity?
7. What can you learn from that person? What is his or her motivation? What is his or her standard for making the choices?

_____

_____

_____

On July 31, 1834, eight hundred thousand slaves in the British Empire were set free. That day was the culmination of a very determined effort, led for more than forty-six years by one man: William Wilberforce.

Wilberforce served in Parliament from 1780 to 1825. During a visit to the Continent in 1785, he noticed that his friend, who was traveling with him, was reading *A Serious Call to a Devout and Holy Life* by William Law. The two men agreed to read and study the book together, and it had a profound impact on Wilberforce's life. As a result, he introduced the first legislation against trading slaves to the House of Commons in 1788.

Wilberforce concluded the three-and-a-half-hour oration with the statement, "Sir, when we think of eternity and the future consequence of all human conduct, what is there in this life that shall make any man contradict the dictates of his conscience, the principles of justice and the law of God!"

Despite that rousing oration, the motion failed.

Wilberforce brought the motion up again every year for eighteen years, until a bill in 1806 finally made the trading of slaves illegal. He then introduced a campaign to abolish slavery altogether in the British Empire, and that bill was passed on July 29, 1833—a full forty-six years later. Four days later, Wilberforce died—his mission accomplished. Almost exactly one year later, the slaves were set free.

> *Opportunity may knock only once, but temptation leans on the doorbell.*
> —UNKNOWN

It took Wilberforce almost half a century to accomplish the task, and it was done in two lengthy stages: first making the trading of slaves illegal, then abolishing slavery itself. That perseverance, in the face of vigorous economic, cultural, and political opposition, is what also set the stage for slavery to be abolished in the United States.[3]

Wilberforce had many opportunities in which he could have given up. He had forty-six years' worth of obstacles!

Take the golden challenge and don't give up. Persevere in doing the good, the right, and the true. You'll benefit, others will benefit, and you won't have to pay the price for choices made out of laziness, convenience, or fear of opposition.

When an archer misses the mark, he turns and looks for the fault within himself. Failure to hit the bull's-eye is never the fault of their target. To improve your aim, improve yourself. —Gilbert Arland

Keep Your Promises
Even When It Hurts

Leaders who win the respect of others are the ones who deliver more than they promise, not the ones who promise more than they can deliver.

—Mark Clement

Driving Thought

The Power of One requires a stubborn determination to do the right thing even in the face of pain.

Drilling Down

Where do you draw the line when it comes to keeping a promise? You probably have no trouble keeping one when it's convenient, like when it's something you want to do anyway.

But what about when keeping the promise inconveniences you, is something that bores you, or requires a big investment of time, money, or emotions? Do you still keep your promises?

Sir Walter Scott kept his promises—even though they were painful to him. You may be familiar with Scott. A biographer, critic, historian, and poet, Scott is considered the father of the historical novel, and he is credited with influencing novelists Leo Tolstoy, Alexandre Dumas, Victor Hugo, Honoré de Balzac, and others.

Scott was born in 1771 in Edinburgh, Scotland. He began his professional life as a lawyer following an apprenticeship under his father, but he soon turned to writing and quickly became the most popular novelist of his day. In 1808, he became a partner in a publishing company, which yielded him greater revenue than simply placing his works with another publisher.

In 1826, his publishing company found itself in financial trouble when it was caught up in another business's bankruptcy. The debt was enormous: £114,000, or about $160,000. Scott probably could have avoided the responsibility for paying the debt by declaring bankruptcy, but he didn't. He had accepted the debt, so he made sure to keep his promise—even though it took him until nearly his death to do so.

Over the next six years, Scott, an already prolific author, wrote mountains of pages to earn money. He sold copyrights. He did whatever he could. In the end, he raised £70,000 before he died. Some people believe he wrote himself to death. But his will gave instructions concerning how additional works could be sold, and the debt was paid. Not only did he not allow pain to stop him from keeping a promise; he would not allow even death to do it.

You don't meet many people like Scott today. Most of us prefer to do what's easy instead of what's right. But if we really want to live a golden life, then we would do well to follow his example.

> *Every civilization rests on a set of promises . . . If the promises are broken too often, the civilization dies, no matter how rich it may be, or how mechanically clever it is. It all comes down to our promises.*
>
> —HERBERT AGAR

SUMMARIZING PRINCIPLES

1. My name and my word are the most important assets I have.

2. Doing the right thing can cost little to nothing—or cost a lot. But the cost shouldn't be the main thing.

3. Sometimes suffering the consequence for doing right acts as a down payment toward building the confidence and trust of others.

MAKING EVALUATION

Charles Brewer, the founder of MindSpring Enterprises, has made promise keeping foundational to his company. When MindSpring was founded in 1993, he included this statement in the company's core values: "We make commitments with care, and then live up to them. In all things, we do what we say we are going to do." He believed that if he could create a business environment where keeping promises was the norm rather than the exception, he would be significantly ahead of the competition.[1]

"Promise made–promise kept" is a very high standard for one person, much less a whole company. But it is so very important. If someone doesn't keep his or her word, then there really is very little basis to build a working relationship upon. A promise not kept is the shifting sands of integrity.

A study conducted by Dr. Pat Lynch was recently published in *The Journal of Business Ethics*. Lynch asked more than seven hundred businesspeople and graduate business students to rank their values in the workplace. Included in addition to promise keeping were such items as competency, work ethic, seniority, and overcoming adversity.

Lynch found that keeping promises was at the bottom of people's lists. That sad statistic held true in the survey regardless of gender, supervisory experience, or religious background. The irony is that promise keeping is the cornerstone of all relationships, and it is absolutely essential for success in business.

1. Is a promise something that only has a legal contract connected to it?
2. Where do you draw the line when it comes to keeping a promise?

_____

_____

_____

_____

3. Do you keep your promises when it is not convenient?
4. Do you keep your promises when it will really hurt?
5. What are some negative effects of failing to keep a promise?

_____

_____

_____

_____

6. What are the benefits of keeping promises?

_____

_____

_____

_____

7. Do you operate with the conviction that your word and having a trusted good name is more important than material fortune?

TAKING ACTION

A promise holds intrinsic value to the one who receives it. Like a certificate of deposit or a stock certificate, it is backed by the resources of the issuer. It's not a flippant comment made in haste. Nor is it a tool to garner trust during a sales pitch—that's a biggie.

> *For every promise, there is a price to pay.*
>
> —E. JAMES ROHN

A promise is a check backed by the resources of our integrity. Here are a few things to consider when making a promise:

Think Before You Speak

Use the *P* word carefully. Count the cost of keeping a promise *before* you make it—not after. Clear communication on your ability to back up what you say will set the proper expectation for those you deal with. Please note: If you feel there's a good chance you'll be unable to fulfill your commitment, then don't promise a fulfillment! Instead, communicate clearly that you are going to try hard to fulfill it, but there is a chance it will not happen. We should make a promise only when we are willing to allocate whatever time and resources it takes to back it up.

- What is one practical way you could implement the "think before you speak" challenge?

_____

_____

_____

Write It Down

If you make a promise, book it in your calendar or to-do list. Give yourself a reminder of your commitment. Quite often we simply get too busy or just plain forget what we promised, even though our intention wasn't to drop the ball. It's a symptom of a busy lifestyle.

- What practical steps can you take to keep your promises? Write them down on the following lines—then put them to use.

_____

_____

_____

_____

_____

Back It Up

Commit to keeping your promises even when it hurts. Are you willing to take a loss to keep your word? If not, then return to step one. If so, then you are well on your way to living out the Power of One.

- How big of a hit are you willing to take to keep a promise?

_____

_____

_____

_____

Do Some Accounting

Do you have any promises outstanding? Have you written any checks on your integrity that need to be backed up? List any promises you have made and then give an action you will take to fulfill each promise:

Promise made	Action to be taken	Date scheduled
1. A fishing trip with my son	Book the trip	Today
2. Free product training for Client XYZ	Do the training	This month
3.		
4.		
5.		
6.		

THE POWER OF ONE

I keep my word and my oath at all costs regardless of the penalty.

1. Always true

2. Sometimes true

3. Rarely true

In 1973, John Naber, an Olympic Gold Medalist swimmer, learned what pain is—and reaped the character rewards of going through that pain. He was competing in the U.S. National Swimming Championships in Kansas City. Because of his six-foot-six-inch height, Naber used a different lap turn than most swimmers—one that allowed him to turn without touching the wall. But that's precisely where the problem occurred.

> *Do not consider painful what is good for you.*
> —EURIPIDES

At the end of his first lap, Naber failed to touch the wall—an infraction. Once he realized it, he doubled back and tapped the wall, but it was too late. An official saw him.

As Naber finished ahead of his competitors, people began congratulating him on his win. They obviously hadn't seen his infraction. However, the referee pulled him aside and disqualified him. Naber's coach offered to fight the ruling, pitting Naber's word against the referee's.

Naber could have argued with the referee—but he has said that he knew he was wrong. In one painful moment, Naber chose to be honest, putting more stock in his character than in winning. He kept a promise to himself, even when it hurt: his promise to be a man of honesty and truth.[2]

Since that day, Naber has said he learned the importance of character—of trustworthiness, responsibility, and citizenship as they apply to swimming and to his life. Fairness, respect, and caring also come into play. And that's the true Power of One.

If asked when you can deliver something, ask for time to think. Build in a margin of safety. Name a date. Then deliver it earlier than you promised. The world is divided into two classes of people: the few people who make good on their promises (even if they don't promise as much), and the many who don't. Get in Column A and stay there. You'll be very valuable wherever you are. —Robert Townsend

---

Day 30

THE FINISH LINE:
GO FOR THE GOLDEN RULE

Do all the good you can, by all the means you can, in all the ways you can, in all the places you can, at all the times you can, to all the people you can, as long as ever you can.

—JOHN WESLEY

DRIVING THOUGHT

The Power of One requires that I focus on the marathon view of life, realizing that a well-done finish is greater than an enthusiastic start.

DRILLING DOWN

Many people enthusiastically romance the idea of running a marathon. They start training, but very few make it through the training periods. Another group will make it to the race—but then won't finish. And a select few will tough it out and cross the finish line—no matter how long it takes them. And if you ask these finishers, they'll tell you it took too long, but they're still full of the sense of self-satisfaction and personal challenge that comes with pushing yourself to succeed. It's that sense of self-achievement that often pushes these people to finish in the first place.

Dick Hoyt, however, was driven by a different fuel tank. The golden spirit of giving—to his own son, nonetheless—pushed him to complete not one, but more than twenty marathons. I know sons can inspire fathers to do great things, but twenty marathons!

Dick Hoyt had the perfect motivation. His son, Rick, has had cerebral palsy since birth—but he never let that stop him from getting involved. When Rick was fifteen, he asked his father if he could participate in a five-kilometer race to benefit an athlete paralyzed in an accident. Dick jerry-rigged a chair to use to push his son in to complete the race. The smile, the gratitude, and the feeling of accomplishment that Rick felt convinced his father to continue on their journey—which they've been doing since 1981.

And about the tendency for marathon runners to think they didn't run fast enough, take note: Dick and Rick Hoyt took sixteen hours and fourteen minutes to finish a race in 1999—and that was an improvement of two hours since their first marathon.

Since that first race, they've participated in every Boston Marathon, an Ironman Triathlon World Championship competition, and various other races throughout the year. Dick doesn't run the races for the awards, the fame, or the prestige. He does it to give something to his son. The finish line lay before him, but the energy to get from start to finish was built on the desire for good, the right, and the true.[1] Dick has the deep hunger to practice the Power of One.

> *Giving frees us from the familiar territory of our own needs by opening our mind to the unexplained worlds occupied by the needs of others.*
>
> —ANNE FRANK

SUMMARIZING PRINCIPLES

1. The golden-ruled life is more of a daily grind than it is a year-end celebration.
2. There is a world of difference between people who go for the gold and those who go for the golden rule.
3. The Golden Path will always be more self-fulfilling and beneficial to mankind than the path of tarnished living.
4. Our culture is in desperate need of a new crop of heroes who live out the good, the right, and the true.
5. The Power of One is one person's ability to have positive influence in any family, any community, and any country, and it should never be minimized.

MAKING EVALUATION

I believe there are two basic paths to achievement a person can choose. You can go for the gold, or you can go for the golden rule.

One path is pretty simple and it looks rather straight. It is the path of self-centered fulfillment—doing anything we want, anytime we want, with no regard for others or the rules of life. It bends and breaks the ethical code of the universe for all kinds of reasons. But in the end, the good, the right, and the true have been overlooked for the bad, the wrong, and the false.

This path appears to be the easy path at first glance. No rocks. No hills to climb. This journey will not even make me sweat, you say to yourself. But along the walk—especially toward the end—it starts getting difficult. You run into problems you never expected on this easy outing.

The other road, the road less traveled, is not always easy. It doesn't even pretend to be easy at first glance. You immediately see the hills, curves, and challenges awaiting you. You know you're going to break a sweat, and the possibility of twisting an ankle is high. But still you do it. And you find it richly fulfilling—something those who take the "easy" path just don't understand. Why is it so satisfying to do the good, the right, and the true?

Because for most of us, the quest to satisfy individual wants and needs is not enough. In *When Everything You Ever Wanted Isn't Enough*, Harold Kushner writes, "Our souls are not hungry for fame, comfort, wealth or power. Our souls are hungry for meaning, for the sense that we have figured out how to live so that our lives matter so that the world will be at least a little bit different for our having passed through it."

Isn't that the truth? If you've ever worked in a less-than-challenging work environment, you'll understand Kushner's writings intimately. There's little worse in a job than putting in your forty hours—with no sense of accomplishment to show for it.

Warren Bennis, an expert on leadership in the corporate world, believes that Americans no longer have any real heroes or outstanding leaders.

Once we admired Lindbergh, DiMaggio, or Astaire because they were examples of excellence; now our heroes are merely the rich and famous who have power, prestige, and lavish lifestyles. In the absence of anything better, we dote on show business stars, idolize corporate kings, and even admire people who have broken the law, slipped into immorality, or dropped out of society. We prefer to read about Madonna rather than Mother Teresa because the nun leaves us feeling shallow and sinful, while the superstar leaves us feeling self-righteous and morally superior.[2]

Our culture is in desperate need of a new crop of heroes. And we know it. Being a hero and being famous are not the same thing. My church is a special place. It is challenging and healthy all at the same time. One of the many things that I love about my church is the attention to platforming the ordinary heroes of life. It has built into its culture the public affirmation of "You are my hero." On any given day I will overhear someone from my church either mentioning that another attendee is his or her hero. Or, even more impressive is the public declaration on the spot of someone looking at

> *A hero is someone we can admire without apology.*
> —KITTY KELLEY

another member and saying, "You are really my hero in this area." We're trying to counter the trend of pop-culture heroes, instead marking the true heroes in our community. After ten years of that kind of affirming, heroes are all over our community.

There is a world of difference between people who go for the gold and those who go for the golden rule:

People Who Go for the Gold . . .	People Who Go for the Golden Rule . . .
• ask, "What can you do for me?"	• ask, "What can I do for you?"
• make convenient decisions.	• make character decisions.
• sacrifice family for finances.	• sacrifice finances for family.
• develop a rationale for their actions.	• develop relationships with their actions.
• possess a "me first" mind-set.	• possess an "others first" mind-set.
• count their dollars.	• count their friends.
• base their values on their worth.	• base their worth on their values.

1. Circle the descriptions above that best describe your mode of operation. On which side do you have more items circled?

2. What are the benefits of living by the golden rule? Why would you go for the gold instead?

_____

_____

_____

_____

_____

3. Can you remember a situation in which you acted according to the golden rule? Describe the experience. How did you and the person you interacted with benefit?

_____

_____

_____

_____

_____

_____

_____

_____

_____

_____

TAKING ACTION

If you choose to practice the Power of One and live out the golden rule, then you should expect to add value to the lives of others. A life lived by the golden rule will create a legacy that far outlives our lives on earth.

How has another person influenced your life? To get you thinking, consider the following:

1. Name three teachers who inspired you to achieve in school.

_____

_____

_____

2. Name three friends who helped you through a difficult time.

_____

_____

_____

3. Name five people who taught you something worthwhile.

_____

_____

_____

_____

_____

4. Name three people who made you feel appreciated and special.

_____

_____

_____

5. Name five people with whom you enjoy spending time.

_____

_____

_____

6. Name half a dozen heroes whose stories have inspired you.

_____

_____

_____

_____

_____

_____

The above-mentioned people have acted out the Power of One in your life! Imagine how many people you could add value to by going for the golden rule. Just think that someday, somewhere, someone could add your name to a similar list. Wouldn't that be great?

Remember, it takes just one person to make a difference in the life of another.

In 1645, one vote gave Oliver Cromwell control of England.

In 1649, one vote caused Charles I of England to be executed.

In 1845, one vote brought Texas into the Union.

In 1868, one vote saved President Andrew Johnson from impeachment.

In 1875, one vote changed France from a monarchy to a republic.

In 1876, one vote gave Rutherford B. Hayes the United States presidency.

In 1923, one vote gave Hitler control of the Nazi party. [3]

Each of us has a single vote to give with our life. It can be either toward influencing others and shaping the Ethical North of any corporate enterprise or it can be directed back toward our own interest and it can ignore the good, the right, and the true. It is up to me. I must not wait around for someone else to cast the vote in practicing the Power of One.

Do I really need to do something? Can't I just wait and let someone else do it? There aren't nearly as many people actually working as you may have thought, at least not according to this survey. Look at this humorous example:

- The population of this country is a little over 250,000,000.

- There are over 84,000,000 people over 64 years of age and retired. That leaves 166,000,000 of us to do all the work.

- People younger than 20 years of age total 95,000,000—so that leaves 71,000,000 to do the work.

- There are 27,000,000 who are employed by the government, which leaves 44,000,000 to do the work. (My apologies to those of you who work for the government. I'll bet you understand.)

- There are 14,000,000 in the armed forces, which leaves 30,000,000 to do all the other work.

- Deduct 20,000,000—the number in state and city offices. That leaves 10,000,000 to do the work.

- There are 6,000,000 in hospitals, mental institutions, and various asylums, so that leaves 4,000,000 to do the work.

- Now it may interest you to know that there are 3,999,998 people in jails and prisons—so that leaves just 2 people to carry the load.

That's you and me—and I'm about ready for a vacation!

OK, that may be pushing it, but you get the point. It's up to you—and me—each one of us to do all that we can do to show the Power of One to others. You never know who's "out on vacation," and when you'll need to pick up their load.

Wayne Alexander and Sam Walton both built their businesses in Bentonville, Arkansas, around the same time. Alexander, a used-car dealer and landlord, came to Bentonville in 1949 and bought his first car lot. Walton, founder of Wal-Mart Stores, Inc., came to Bentonville within a year of Alexander and built his company to be the world's biggest retailer.

Both men loved business, and both men valued a hard

> *Yesterday is a canceled check: Forget it. Tomorrow is a promissory note: Don't count on it. Today is ready cash: Use it!*
>
> —EDWIN C. BLISS

work ethic and spent very little on themselves. But their attitudes toward business were greatly different and the fruit of their lives seems very different.

Walton knew how to invest in the future. He had a great idea for a company, and he planned for it every step of the way. He focused on slim profit margins and selling high margins of products to make his money. He worked hard to make his Wal-Mart stores clean and attractive—while working out of a nice, but modest, office building.

Sam Walton died in 1992. Today, two CEOs removed from its founder, Wal-Mart hails as the largest company in the world. Although not every person in the entire world is happy with Wal-Mart, they have clearly revolutionized the globe. Walton's guiding principles were to think and behave around the good, the right, and the true. He was paying it forward, and it has grown into a worldwide harvest.[4]

Alexander, a man in his seventies who still works six days a week to make a living, grew his business quite differently. He refuses to reinvest any of the money he earns into cleaning up his properties. He has taken a more narrow view of life's pursuits. The city has leveled at least one of the apartment buildings he owns because of its dilapidated condition, and people have brought lawsuits against him for the same issue. Alexander seems to operate on a different path than Sam Walton did. Two very different men with two different paths. Each man, just as we are, was given the chance to practice the Power of One. What an apparent contrast in two lives.

We all have one lifetime to live. Some people have twenty-five years. Some have a hundred. What matters is how we use those years, months, weeks, and days.

The Power of One calls on each one of us to enter the marathon and not quit when we get tired or the path becomes challenging.

The smallest good deed is better than the grandest intention.

Golden Challenges

Need a little help honing your ethical skills? Try your hand at these Golden Challenges, so named because they give you a chance to use the golden rule when dealing with others. How would you handle these sticky situations?

1. Supermarket Showdown

You are the manager at the local grocery store, and you run an ad in the paper proclaiming, "Lean ground beef, $2.12/lb." The next day, you're called to the front where an angry customer shows you that the meat is actually marked $0.12/lb, and explains that she feels the cashier should not charge her the $2.12 price because it is the store's fault for mispricing. She is obviously attempting to take advantage of your mistake and has eight packs (nearly 20 pounds) of ground beef in her shopping cart. What should you do?

2. Two Left Feet

One of your feet is slightly bigger than the other, and as long as you can remember, only one of your shoes fits and the other is either extremely tight or very loose. You run a lot to exercise, and because one of your shoes never fits, you consistently sprain ankles and get blisters. Whenever you pick out a new pair of running shoes, you consider taking one shoe out of two separate boxes. You have mentioned the problem to the manager several times, hoping he could help you out, but he's never given you a direct answer. You're in the store, and they have plenty of pairs of the shoe you want in both sizes you need. What should you do?

3. I'll Fly Away

Several months ago, you canceled a flight that you had reserved with your credit card, and you received your money back, but the frequent flyer miles that you earned when you purchased the flight stayed on your account. The next time you went to the airport, you asked the woman at the ticket counter, but she neither knew what you should do nor did she consider it a major issue. You fly regularly and are considering booking flights whenever a trip is a vague possibility, thinking that, if you need to cancel, you can keep the frequent flyer miles. What should you do?

4. Buckle Up

You serve twice a month at a local church, driving vans to pick up kids who live within three miles of the church. You've been picking up the same kids for two years, and you just learned of the child safety seat law, which requires child seats for nearly one-third of the kids you pick up. Some of the children have been riding with you for two years without these seats and would throw a fit if you tried to force them to ride in seats. Not only do you not have any child seats, but some of the kids are within a couple of months and/or a couple of pounds of not needing the safety seats. You never let them sit in the front, and you are rarely on busy streets, but does that matter? What should you do?

5. My Boss's Keeper

During a routine company meeting, one of your coworkers announces that the boss has purposefully put off raises and bonuses for the vast majority of employees. The forty employees in the room (many of whom you rarely see and hardly know) quickly begin to verbally bash the boss. Later that afternoon, your coworker tells you that he made up the story about your boss. While you have never known your boss to be especially employee-friendly, you feel bad that your boss is getting an undeserved bad reputation. What should you do?

6. Mr. Postman

Your company has a mail meter that allows employees to pay postage without using stamps. You and your family live so far from the post office that you never have time to go get stamps on your own, and you've gotten into the habit of using the postage machine whenever you have a bill or something else that has to be mailed in quickly. You're not the only person in the company who does this, and some employees talk as if the right to use the postage machine is a job perk. What should you do?

7. Try and Try Again?

Somehow your bank gave you an extra $1,000 on a recent deposit, and it was the end of the month before you noticed the error. You called the bank and later visited in person to explain the situation and show the incorrect deposit ticket. It's now been more than six months and you still have the extra $1,000 in your account. You really don't have time to keep going by the bank, so you're thinking about giving the $1,000 to a local charity. What should you do?

8. An Ounce of Prevention . . .

You work for a small company that is planning to offer a new service that no other businesses currently offer. In interviewing for a job with another company, however, you learned that this other company (a much larger one than your current company) will begin offering the same service within the month. While you signed no contract, it seemed that they were telling you this in confidence. Your current company could lose thousands of dollars and several jobs if their new venture flops. If you tell them now, you might be able to keep that from happening. What should you do?

9. The Truth, The Whole Truth

You've interviewed for several jobs but haven't even received a call back yet. Then, one afternoon, you interview with a local company that seems very interested. As you're discussing the position, the manager says, "We sometimes have a hard time finding employees because we require a two-year commitment from them." You know that your husband's job has the potential to require him to move, but he hasn't moved in the last four years. You're optimistic that you won't need to move in the next two years, but you could never be sure. What should you do?

10. A Manager in Entry-Level Clothing

You're preparing your résumé for a round of job interviews, and you have to list your previous job titles and duties. While you've never been beyond entry-level, your last job was in a small office, and you had to be versatile enough to occasionally be in charge—making decisions, representing the company at meetings, and so forth—while the boss was gone for a day or week at a time. The way to best represent this on your résumé is to give yourself a higher position than you really had. Your current interviews are with much larger companies, and you want to make sure they know that you can handle more than entry-level work. What should you do?

11. Downtime

There are a lot of times at your job when there's really not much to do. During those times, you've gotten into the habit of closing the door to your office and working on a book you're writing on your own time. You only do this after you've finished everything the boss has given you. Should you continue to do this?

12. New Guy

Your company recently hired a new tech guy, and by all accounts, he was not a good hire. The other employees from the tech department consistently make fun of him, and your coworkers complain that their problems aren't fixed when he "repairs" their computers. The last time he helped you, you had to call someone else to fix your computer after he couldn't solve the problem. You overheard your boss saying that he was considering letting him go. Your coworkers are now purposely requesting other tech workers, even if the new guy is right there and says he knows what to do. This morning, you had yet another computer problem, and the new guy is just down the hall. What should you do?

13. Don't Call Me; I'll Call You

You have a company cell phone, and you've gotten into the habit of giving that number out as your second number since it's always with you. Without really trying to, you're starting to receive nearly as many personal calls on that phone as business calls. What should you do?

14. School Ties

You are the boss of a small company, and one of your employees lives in the country several miles away. She works overtime several days a week and often brings in her son to work after he finishes preschool. In filling out forms for her son to go to elementary school in the fall, she asks you if she can use the office as her main address. This would allow her son to go to the top elementary school in town, rather than the worst school. She says she could drop him off in the morning, and he could ride the bus back to the office after school. It would be no burden on anyone in the office and would certainly benefit the boy's education. What should you do?

15. Good Advice

Your stockbroker also works for some of the higher-ups at a highly prominent and highly successful mutual fund manager. Your broker has offered to let you know, in general terms, what stocks these investors are buying and selling. How should you respond to this offer?

16. Doctor's Visit

You evaluate patients for a large health insurance company. It is company policy that if a patient's condition has existed for more than three months before he or she seeks treatment, the company will not pay for it. Patients, however, do not know this policy and often turn in claims that are more than three months old. Usually, these patients simply did not think their problems warranted a doctor's visit until now. If you fudge the dates on their medical records, they can receive treatment, but if you are honest, they will most likely be turned down. What should you do?

17. Help Yourself

Sometimes you work on business projects at home, so you occasionally bring home a five-hundred-sheet ream of paper. Usually, this paper ends up being used for personal work, however, such as your son's schoolwork and your Christmas newsletters. No one at work has ever said anything for or against employees taking paper or other supplies. What should you do?

18. Justifying the Means?

You are heavily involved in a fund-raising drive for the local hospital. Recently, you received two large checks from a company currently under suspicion for tax evasion, wire fraud, and various accounting scandals. If you refuse the money, it is highly doubtful the hospital will meet its goal. What should you do?

19. Dinner Out

On a recent business trip, you went out to eat with two coworkers and three college friends who live in the area. Your conversation is widespread but never really touches on work. When the check comes, you pull out your wallet, intending to put it on the company credit card. What should you do?

20. Babysitter Troubles

Your regular babysitter is great with your two young children and regularly encourages them to be kind, share, and so forth. Last week, however, you saw her steal a sweater at a local store. You have never had a better babysitter, but you are concerned about the example she is setting for your children. What should you do? Fire her?

21. Getting It Free

You take advantage of every possible promotion that you can find to get free stuff—even though you never have any intention of keeping the stuff you buy. For example, you apply and get all kinds of charge cards so you can get the free miles. You apply to purchase a condo in town just because the condo company is giving away a nice stereo if you tour the property. My friend says this practice is too close to lying and stealing for him. Is it OK?

NOTES

Day 2: Wanted: One Ethical Leader

1. www.time.com/time/personoftheyear/2002/poycooper3.html.

2. "World-Class Scandal at WorldCom," www.cbsnews.com, 26 June 2002.

3. Charles R. Swindoll, *Swindoll's Ultimate Book of Illustrations and Quotes* (Nashville: Thomas Nelson, 2003) 274.

4. Glen Van Ekeren, *Speakers Sourcebook II* (New Jersey: Prentice Hall, 1994), 132.

5. Ibid., 133.

6. Ibid., 135.

Day 3: The Ethical Dilemma

1. "Sen. Torricelli Quits Race," www.newsmax.com, 21 November 2002.

2. Keith H. Hammonds, "Harry Kraemer's Moment of Truth," *Fast Company*, November 2002, 96.

3. John C. Knapp, "Why Business Ethics Is Worthy of Discussion," *Atlanta Business Chronicle*, 18 November 2002.

4. Joseph Fletcher, *Situation Ethics: The New Morality* (Philadelphia: Westminster, 1966).

5. Quoted in *World Magazine*, 7 September 2002, 14.

Day 5: One Rule for Everyone

1. Glen Van Ekeren, *Speakers Sourcebook II* (New Jersey: Prentice Hall, 1994), 319.

2. Matthew 7:12.

3. *The Traditions of Mohammed*, quoted at www.thegoldenrule.net, 23 September 2002.

4. *Talmud*, Shabbat 1a, quoted in "The Universality of the Golden Rule in World Religions," www.teachingvalues.com, 23 September 2002.

5. Udana-Varga 5, 1, quoted in ibid.

6. Mahabharata 5, 1517, quoted in ibid.

7. Shast-na-shayast 13:29, quoted at www.goldenrule.net, 23 September 2002.

8. Analects 15:23, quoted at ibid.

9. Epistle to the Son of the Wolf, 30, quoted at www.fragrant.demon.co.uk/golden, 23 September 2002.

10. Sutrakitanga 1.11.33, quoted at ibid.

11. Ibid.

Day 6: One Rule for Everything

1. *Speakers Sourcebook II*, 319.

Day 7: Most People Accept the Golden Rule

1. Ira Wolfman, "Class Action," *Reader's Digest*, October 2003, 76–79.

2. Tim Sanders, *Love Is the Killer App* (New York: Three Rivers Press, 2002), 168.

3. Ibid., 169–70.

Day 9: The Golden Rule Is a Win-Win Philosophy

1. Art Boulay, "Malden Mills: A Study in Leadership," *Quality Monitor Newsletter*, October 1996.

2. Ibid.

3. "Americans Speak: Enron, WorldCom and Others Are Result of Inadequate Moral Training by Families," 22 July 2002, Barna Research Online, www.barna.org.

4. John C. Knapp, "Why Business Ethics Is Worthy of Discussion," *Atlanta Business Chronicle*, 18 November 2002, Atlanta.bizjournals.com/Atlanta.

5. Joe Griffith, *Speakers Library of Quotes, Stories, Anecdotes and Humor* (New Jersey: Prentice Hall, 1990) 102.

Day 11: The Golden Zone

1. "Corporate Profile," www.synovus.com, 27 January 2003.

Day 13: I Want to Be Trusted

1. Amie Devero, "Corporate Values," *Financial Executive*, May 2003, 21, www.fei.org.

2. Stephen Graves and Thomas Addington, *Clout* (San Francisco: Jossey Bass, 2003), 197.

Day 14: I Want to Be Respected

1. Jokes taken from Rodney.com jokes of the month for October.

Day 15: I Want to Be Understood

1. Andrea Cooper, "A Wing and a Prayer," *Reader's Digest*, March 2003, 91–95.
2. Stuart Levine, *Dr. Seuss* (Lucent Books, 2003).
3. Ibid.

Day 16: I Don't Want Others to Take Advantage of Me

1. TIME 100: Leaders and Revolutionaries; www.nobel.se/peace/laureates/1983/walesa-bio.html.

Day 17: Talent Is a Gift; Character Is a Choice

1. Greg Farrell, "HealthSouth Founder Faces 85 Counts," *USA Today*, 5 November 2003.
2. Charles Swindoll, *Living on the Ragged Edge* (Dallas, TX: Word Publishing, 1985), 275.

Day 18: Pressure Can Tarnish the Golden Touch

1. Gary R. Collins, *You Can Make a Difference: 14 Principles for Influencing Lives* (Grand Rapids, Mich.: Zondervan, 1992), 17–18.
2. Catherine Valenti, "Ethical Culture," abcnews.com, 20 February 2002.
3. Dennis and Barbara Rainey, *Parenting Today's Adolescent* (Nashville: Thomas Nelson, 1998), 57.

Day 22: Priorities Can Tarnish the Golden Touch

1. Amie Devero, "Corporate Values," *Financial Executive*, May 2003.
2. Bonnie Angelo, *First Mothers* (William-Morris, 2000).

Day 23: Ask Others to Hold You Accountable for Your Actions

1. Stephen Graves and Thomas Addington, *Clout* (San Francisco: Jossey Bass, 2003), 73–74.

Day 26: Walk the Second Mile

1. Helen O'Neil, "Dad's Dying Gift to His Kids: A New Family," *Arkansas Democrat Gazette*, (AP) 31 August 2003.
2. Ibid.

Day 27: Help People Who Can't Help You

1. "Eugenio Monti," www.olympic.org/uk/passion/humanity, 25 February 2003.

2. Bernice Selden, *The Story of Annie Sullivan* (Milwaukee, Wis.: Gareth Stevens Publishing, 1997).

Day 28: Do Right When It's Natural to Do Wrong

1. Charles Colson, *Loving God* (Grand Rapids, Mich.: Zondervan, 1983), 27.

2. Peggy Noonan, *When Character Was King* (New York: Viking Press, 2001), 221.

3. Garth Lean, *God's Politician* (Colorado Springs: Helmers & Helmers, 1987).

Day 29: Keep Your Promises Even When It Hurts

1. Ellwood F. Oakley III, "Promise-Keeping Has Lost Its Importance as a Core Value," *Atlanta Business Chronicle*, 18 November 2002.

2. John Naber, "Building Character," *Swimming World and Junior Swimmer*, June 1998, 39–41.

Day 30: The Finish Line: Go for the Golden Rule

1. CNN.com, 29 November 1999.

2. Gary R. Collins, *You Can Make a Difference*, 36.

3. Chuck Swindoll, *Ultimate Book of Illustrations and Quotes* (Nashville: Thomas Nelson, 1998), 297.

4. Christopher Leonard, "Mr. Wayne: Nobody's Millionaire," *Arkansas Democrat-Gazette*, 26 October 2003.

About the Authors

John C. Maxwell is the founder of a nonprofit international Christian leadership organization called EQUIP (Encouraging Qualities Undeveloped in People). This foundation equips international Christian leaders through conferences, resources, partnerships, and technology. For more than twenty-five years Maxwell was a local church senior pastor, most recently at one of America's largest churches. In 1985, he founded INJOY, an organization dedicated to helping people maximize their personal and leadership potential. Each year Maxwell speaks in person to more than 350,000 people and influences the lives of another one million through seminars, books, and tapes. He is the author of more than thirty books, including *Developing the Leader Within You*, *Developing the Leaders Around You*, *Your Road Map for Success*, *The 21 Irrefutable Laws of Leadership*, and *The 17 Indisputable Laws of Teamwork*.

Stephen R. Graves and Thomas G. Addington have been business partners and best friends for almost two decades. For the last fifteen years, they have been exploring how to blend business excellence with biblical wisdom through consulting, teaching, mentoring, and writing. This mission statement, originally scratched out on a breakfast napkin early one morning twelve years ago, has been their "never lost" system as they have journeyed through a variety of entrepreneurial endeavors and experiments. They founded Cornerstone Consulting Group and the *Life@Work Journal*; they speak regularly in business, ministry, and academic settings; they publish frequently; serve on national boards; and they are active in coaching leaders toward the finish line. Both hold earned doctorates, both are deeply devoted to their families, and both love the never-ending challenge of meshing real life with the message of Jesus. They have authored fifteen books or booklets.

OTHER TITLES BY JOHN C. MAXWELL

Developing the Leaders Around You

Developing the Leader Within You

The Maxwell Leadership Bible

The 17 Indisputable Laws of Teamwork

The 17 Essential Qualities of a Team Player

The 21 Indispensable Qualities of a Leader

The 21 Irrefutable Laws of Leadership

Your Road Map for Success

Relationships 101

Equipping 101

Attitude 101

Leadership 101

OTHER TITLES BY STEPHEN GRAVES
AND THOMAS ADDINGTON

Deep Focus:
Devotions for Living the Word

Behind the Bottom Line:
Powering Business Life with Spiritual Wisdom

Life@Work on Leadership:
Enduring Insights for Men and Women of Faith

Daily Focus:
Daily Readings for Integrating Faith in the Workplace

The Building Block Series

Framing Your Ambition

The Hard Work of Rest

Cornerstones for Calling

Ethical Anchors

The Mentoring Blueprint

The Fourth Frontier:
Exploring the New World of Work

The Cornerstones for Life at Work

A Case for Character

A Case for Calling

A Case for Skill

A Case for Serving

ALLOW JOHN C. MAXWELL TO MENTOR YOU MONTHLY.

Maximum Impact Club

Each monthly leadership lesson is designed to challenge, equip and motivate you as you continue on your leadership journey. Thousands of leaders look forward to receiving John C. Maxwell's monthly leadership lessons and building their resource library.

Each membership includes the monthly leadership lesson program and a FREE library-quality storage album. Plus, you qualify for discounts on many Maximum Impact® resources! Membership is only $12 a month.

Available on audiocassette or CD
www.maximumimpact.com/mentoring
877-225-3311

For more information or to subscribe, visit
www.maximumimpact.com/mentoring
or call **877-225-3311**

maximumimpact®

www.maximumimpact.com

THERE'S ONLY ONE RULE
FOR MAKING DECISIONS

The Power of One
TRAINING CURRICULUM

Just what is right and wrong, exactly? In a world of shifting standards, is there an absolute truth to better guide our behavior? Though some politicians and business leaders apparently say "no," John Maxwell says emphatically, "yes!" In *The Power of One* Training Curriculum, Dr. John C. Maxwell shares his wisdom and expertise in running an ethical life and organization. The concept is simple and universal. No more guesswork—just a simple foundation for all internal and external motivation. Personal ethics are becoming the new standard for decision-making in business today. **Give your organization a head start with this training series as you learn to:**

- Define and explain ethics for those in your organization
- Create a larger ROI in terms of trust, respect, and influence
- Identify golden opportunities that arise from ethical decision-making
- Avoid temptations that can tarnish you, your team, and your organization
- Reproduce your standards in others

Want to set a straight path for your feet and ensure your organization's success at the same time? This training series shows you how.

**Call 877-225-3311 or visit www.maximumimpact.com
to order your curriculum today.**

www.maximumimpact.com

THERE'S ONLY ONE RESOURCE TO TEACH IT TO YOUR ORGANIZATION

Targeting business leaders' needs, this course empowers you to:

- Establish an ethical standard from which your organization can operate

- Communicate clearly the code of conduct to veteran and new employees

- Train managers and department heads to create unity in values

Package Contents:

- *Four, 10-minute sessions*
- *2 DVD discs or 2 VHS tapes*
- *1 Facilitator Guide*
- *1 Participant Guide*

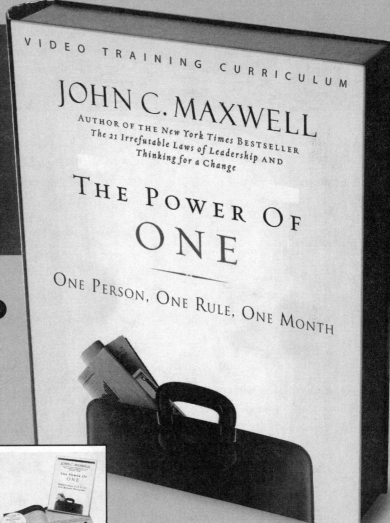

VIDEO TRAINING CURRICULUM

JOHN C. MAXWELL
AUTHOR OF THE *New York Times* BESTSELLER
The 21 Irrefutable Laws of Leadership AND
Thinking for a Change

THE POWER OF ONE

ONE PERSON, ONE RULE, ONE MONTH

877-225-3311

SPEAKER SERVICES

maximumimpact®
SPEAKERS

You need a dynamic and engaging speaker, one with relevant and results-oriented material that will truly impact the way your company does business. You need a speaker that will instruct & inspire your audience; one that will be a catalyst for change within your organization. You need someone who has the power to take your team to higher levels of leadership and performance than you ever imagined.

With keynote, half-day and full-day presentations, Maximum Impact Speakers present leadership, teamwork and personal growth programs designed to fit your organizations needs.

Today matters. If you want to ignite change within your organization and create a culture of Leadership, Teamwork and Personal Growth, don't wait - **schedule your Maximum Impact Speaker today!**

Visit www.maximumimpact.com/speakers
to view our entire roster.

www.maximumimpact.com

BEGIN WITH A FREE CD

Continue to develop the principles of *The Power of One.*

We have made the next step as simple and inexpensive as possible –

It's FREE!

Visit us at www.thepowerofonebook.com for a free CD of Best-Selling author John C. Maxwell, sharing his wisdom and expertise in running an ethical life and organization.

www.thepowerofonebook.com

877-225-3311

, A TRAINING OPPORTUNITY YOU AND THE PEOPLE YOU LEAD.

Maximum Impact Training

What if you could craft a training program to truly meet the ongoing complexities of management while simultaneously benefiting employees with emerging leadership skills? Maximum Impact has the answer in customized training solutions for you and your team in the areas of Leadership, Teamwork and Personal Growth.

John C. Maxwell says, "Leaders are developed daily, not in a day." The change in daily behavior is where leaders and their companies realize their most rewarding gains. Where most corporate training focuses on Job Knowledge and Management Skills, Maximum Impact Training targets the practices and predictable behaviors of great leadership.

Miles beyond self-directed study, marginal video enrichment or the large impersonal group settings you may be used to, you'll find Maximum Impact Training to be a powerful perspective on the most urgent training needs today. Workshops are an interactive exchange led by engaging facilitators. A chance for you and your people to interact with other leaders who are as intentional about personal and professional growth as you are.

m
Leadership Behavior
Management Skills
Job Knowledge

ACT NOW!

Bring Maximum Impact Training to your company!

Call us toll-free at *877-225-3311*

www.maximumimpact.com